AMERICAN
PATRIOTS
IN
PRAYER

AMERICAN
PATRIOTS
IN
PRAYER

THE REBIRTH OF ONE NATION UNDER GOD

DAVID HAMER

Pleasant Word
A Division of WINEPRESS PUBLISHING

Pleasant Word (a division of WinePress Publishing, PO Box 428, Enumclaw, WA 98022) functions only as book publisher. As such, the ultimate design, content, editorial accuracy, and views expressed or implied in this work are those of the author.

Unless otherwise noted, all Scripture quotations are taken from the *New King James Version*. Copyright © 1982 by Thomas Nelson, Inc. Used by permission. All rights reserved.

Scripture quotations marked KJV are taken from the *King James Version* of the Bible.

Scripture references marked NASB are taken from the New American Standard Bible, © 1960, 1963, 1968, 1971, 1972, 1973, 1975, 1977 by The Lockman Foundation. Used by permission.

ISBN 13: 978-1-4141-1197-1
ISBN 10: 1-4141-1197-5
Library of Congress Catalog Card Number: 2008902103

To Carolyn: a cherished gift and a precious treasure. Only Scripture is sufficient to express your beauty and articulate the inner riches your godly character radiates: "Who can find a virtuous woman? For her price is far above rubies."

(Prov. 31:10 KJV)

CONTENTS

PREFACE

In the end, we will remember not the words of our enemies, but the silence of our friends.
                                        —Martin Luther King, Jr.

I FEAR GOD'S displeasure if I were to remain silent more than I fear the criticism of those who will judge me for publishing this pointed, prophetic ultimatum. It is only right that I should forewarn you: you may find some of the probing and provocative truths that follow difficult to read. Why?

This book was written to confront the Christianized humanism of me-first spirituality that is epidemic throughout the church in America. Multitudes of believers have been infected and weakened with this low-impact, high-maintenance distortion of Christianity. Self-surrender that embraces the cross is the very heart of authentic Christian discipleship. In these pages, I vigorously challenge the gospel of self-fulfillment that has ensnared American Christians in spiritual indifference. It is our failure to live sacrificially as disciples that has enfeebled the church, leaving her culturally impotent. The spiritual decline of the United States is rooted in the prayerlessness of God's church.

Our country's spiritual restoration will only begin if sweeping repentance in God's church stirs multitudes to rebuild the altars of fervent prayer.

This book exposes the looming judgment our nation will tragically and most certainly incur if American believers fail to unite in sweeping repentance and selfless, kingdom-advancing prayer. The words you will read on these pages were fearfully and prayerfully written to convey God's sobering call to all believers in America to fall on their knees—before cataclysmic judgment for our national sin suddenly comes. This divine call to repentance and prayer is inclusive of every blood-bought believer in every church, in every denomination, in every city and village across America. I pray that through this book many will hear God calling them to prayer. More directly to the point, I pray that *you* will hear Him calling *you*.

Does my direct approach seem insensitive to you? The urgent call upon these pages was not written to *condemn* you, but neither was it written to *comfort* you. Rather, this book was written to *compel* you. These words of truth are frightening but hopeful. This proclamation confronts the frail forms of comfortable Christianity that have handicapped the church in America. This book condemns our national sin of abortion, while it reveals how the massacre of more than fifty million unborn children has brought our country to the very brink of destruction.

Constrained by prophetic insight and commissioned with a prophetic duty, I am urgently pleading with every American Christian to unite in repentance and prayer in order to heal the slashed heart and bleeding womb of our dying nation, lest we reap the ominous harvest of mass murder that we have savagely sown. This message conveys a God-given urgency, because time to heal Lady Liberty from abortion's mortal wound is quickly running out. And yet few seem to comprehend this—even now at the very brink of national ruin!

My heart does ache for the sons and daughters of America who have lost a child through abortion. I want to make it clear that, in this book, I am not addressing individuals nor the spiritual and emotional aftermath that terminating a pregnancy buries in a ravaged soul and entombs in a haunted heart. The sharp pen I used to compose this message was not chosen to cut *you* again, this time with words, if you made the tragic choice to abort your baby. This piercing outcry against our national atrocity should not be misconstrued as malice toward you. The furthest thing from my heart is to stab you with condemnation, bruise you with contempt, or wound you with the cutting declaration contained in this shrill forewarning. Far from it!

Because of His unconditional love for you, Jesus was wounded for your transgressions and bruised for your iniquities. He was condemned to die and pierced on a bloody cross to purchase *your* soul's salvation. If your heart still bears the guilt of abortion, humble yourself in repentance and cry out to God for mercy until He softly speaks words of forgiveness to your scarred heart. Linger in remorse at the foot of the cross until godly sorrow leads you to the joy of redeeming grace. Then the Holy Spirit will gently whisper to you that all is well with your soul.

I also want my readers to understand that I am not wielding this sword in judgment of those who brandish the brazen scalpels of slaughter. I pray that these executioners of the innocent unborn would drop their cold-blooded surgical weapons, run toward God, and fall on their knees in repentance before Him to find mercy for their grievous sins. Those doctors of death who do not will ultimately face the God of life and His eternal judgment for the crimes against humanity they have ruthlessly committed. I pray that the God of infinite mercy will grant them repentance before they stand before Him eternally stained with innocent shed blood and without hope on the dreadful Day of Judgment.

The warped souls who bomb clinics, threaten their workers, or shoot abortionists will not find an ally in these pages. Those demented anarchists deserve to reap the consequences the courts are empowered to execute for their lawless behavior. Vicious acts of violence against the unborn in the slaughterhouses are the problem. More violent acts or threats by extremist radicals at the clinics of abortionists are not the solution. It is impossible to promote life by malevolence, murder, and mayhem. The real war being waged is not against abortionists in their chambers of death. We are in a spiritual conflict against "principalities and powers, the rulers of the darkness of this world, and spiritual wickedness in high places" (Eph. 6:12) for the unborn innocents and the lost soul and bleeding womb of our erring nation. Rather than inflaming perverted passions by advocating violence, all genuine pro-life people need to ignite their hearts in prevailing prayer as they passionately plead for God's mercy. Together, on our knees, we must seek forgiveness—even for the doctors of death whom these misled militants rabidly abhor. Death, hatred, and violence are the adversaries of life. *American Patriots in Prayer* rejects all of the deceived fanatics who claim to be fighting for life while the same spirit of death, hatred, and violence that spawned abortion seethes in their savage souls.

All true American believers in all denominations must hear the word of the Lord. America is facing a grave harvest of death and devastation at the hands of brutal terrorists because we have sown the slaughter of fifty million unborn babies. With the shedding of our children's blood, we have made a blood covenant with death that is empowering hell to destroy America. Demonic powers are the instigators that use vicious human souls perverted in hatred as the facilitators of terrorist attacks against the United States. These attacks will continue and escalate until we repent from the terrorism of aborting the helpless, innocent unborn.

There are no military or political solutions that can save us from reaping a terrifying harvest from the ripening seeds of death we have so viciously sown. But God's Word *does* reveal a cure for Lady Liberty's bloodthirsty curse. If American Christians from all denominations mobilize in repentance and prayer, abounding grace can yet redeem us from the guilt of our holocaust. Astonishing mercy can rescind the menacing reckoning that looms over our desecrated land. Indeed, there are only two possible futures for American civilization. Both of them are very bloody. The first frightful fate is a bloodbath of vengeance for our massacre of the unborn innocents. The only alternative is a redeeming bloodbath of repentance at the foot of the rugged cross.

This book reveals the mortal wound abortion has inflicted upon our nation and hell's succeeding threefold strategy to destroy our country. It also reveals our solemn responsibility as American Christians to diligently pray for a wave of national repentance and an American spiritual awakening. Consider God's glorious promise of pardon, cleansing, and restoration:

> *If My people who are called by My name will humble themselves, and pray and seek My face, and turn from their wicked ways, then I will hear from heaven, and will forgive their sin and heal their land.*
>
> (2 Chron. 7:14)

The twenty-first century church holds the destiny of the United States in her hands. In prevailing prayer or in complacent indifference, God's church will choose America's future: repentance leading to a spiritual awakening—or a grim reaping of terror, leading to national ruin. I pray that the Holy Spirit will use the frightening but hopeful forewarning in this book to awaken a multitude of believers in the slumbering church. Before the darkness falls on the black night of our country's catastrophic reckoning, we must mobilize a multitude of American patriots in prayer. The clock to national judgment is ticking fast. Let us immediately join forces and wage war on our knees, until God grants us the rebirth of one nation under God!

INTRODUCTION:
AMERICA, FALL ON ℰ
YOUR KNEES!

O LORD, I have heard thy speech, and was afraid: O LORD, revive thy work in the midst of the years, in the midst of the years make known; in wrath, remember mercy.

—Habakkuk 3:2

THE PROPHETIC POEM that follows was written on my heart twelve years before the 9/11 attacks. At that time, my wife, Carolyn, and I were traveling across the nation in a prophetic teaching ministry to the body of Christ. After a very difficult meeting at a fellowship where we were scheduled to speak two more times, I spent about two hours in intercessory prayer before going to bed. I was seeking God for a spiritual breakthrough in this congregation in the two remaining meetings.

The next morning, as soon as I awoke, I sought God again in lingering worship and fervent prayer. Then I sat down with my Bible and a pen and paper to begin working on my message for the evening gathering. As I picked up my pen, an enveloping presence of God entered the room as the prophetic message "America, Fall on Your Knees" was imparted to my spirit. The weighty, rhythmic, poetic words of this prophecy rose up out of my spirit into my mind as fast as I was able to scribble them down on paper.

In just a few minutes this prophetic poem was completed. I did not mull over it to find just the right words, nor did I adjust the perfect cadence in any way. I am convinced that it was the Holy Spirit dictating God's thoughts directly from the Father's heart to my trembling soul. I have never written anything in that manner before or since. In almost forty years as a Christian, nothing but my conversion experience itself has ever impacted me as profoundly and indelibly as that divine encounter. The dreadful sensing of God's presence and my fearful insight into God's heart left me trembling in holy awe. Those few moments in God's presence, more than twenty years ago, altered my entire life. That morning God forged the focus of my divine destiny. I was born to cry out against America's national sin, declaring God's ultimatum of national repentance or national ruin. America will soon experience the consuming fury of divine wrath, unless multitudes cry out in repentance to seek mercy, forgiveness, and a divine restoration.

As soon as I recorded these poetic words on my notepad, I heard the Lord say clearly: "*I have given you a prophetic lament for America.*" This grave message, warning of impending wrath, also revealed the conditional promise that repentance and prayer could obtain God's mercy, leading to an American spiritual restoration. Almost immediately, the music for this lamentation followed, as did a vision of the Statue of Liberty in tears, kneeling with her broken torch.

The rest of my life will be dedicated to seeing the wrath averted and the restoration apprehended that this prophecy proclaims. As the prophet declared, "O LORD, I have heard thy speech, and was afraid: O LORD, revive thy work in the midst of the years; in wrath, remember mercy" (Hab. 3:2).

America, Fall on Your Knees!

Who would have believed? What mind could have conceived?
America, land of desolations!
What has happened unto thee, the sweet Land of Liberty?
The envy of all the other nations....
Where's the vision that was thine when your forefathers signed,
For independence, their bold Declaration?
When godliness was revered, I was honored, loved, and feared.
With My blessing you became a mighty nation.

Once the Land of the Free, once the Home of the Brave,
We have forsaken the Living God, in whose image we were made.
If to Him we will return, from His wrath He may yet turn.
America, fall on your knees!

By the sweat of the slaves' brows were your cotton fields all plowed.
Like oxen, herded onto your plantations.
By the slaves that you owned, were the seeds of Civil War sown,
As they cried out to Me in desperation.
They shed blood, sweat, and tears by your injustices for years,
Till I arose in My indignation.
I smote your land with the sword, for this brutality I abhorred.
With your blood I brought Emancipation.

Once the Land of the Free, once the Home of the Brave,
We have forsaken the Living God, in whose image we were made.
If to Him we will return, from His wrath He may yet turn.
America, fall on your knees!

Up from the ground I again hear the sound
Of innocent blood being shed in your nation.
It's the cry of the unborn, from their mothers' wombs they're torn
As they gasp for life in desperation.
What is this that thou hast done?

They're your daughters. They're your sons.
My greatest gift, the crown of My creation.
I am girding on My sword. These ruthless murders I abhor.
I will smite again your blood-guilty nation.

Once the Land of the Free, once the Home of the Brave,
We have forsaken the Living God in whose image we were made.
If to Him we will return, from His wrath He may yet turn.
America, fall on your knees!

Why are My people still asleep? I behold you and I weep.
The only hope of your dying nation!
Unaware of gathering gloom, Apart from you, America's doomed.
Church of God, where is your consecration?
By your pleasures you're still bound. On your knees you're rarely found,
Crying out with tears and supplications.
For her sins My fury's stored. By the church, I'm still ignored.
Shall I come in wrath, or restoration?

Once the Land of the Free, once the Home of the Brave,
We have forsaken the Living God in whose image we were made.
If to Him we will return, from His wrath He may yet turn.
America, fall on your knees!

After receiving this poetic prophecy, I continued to travel nationwide for another six years with a limited platform to call the church to prayer and repentance for the horrifying abomination of abortion that was sowing the seeds of destruction into our blood-guilty land. The word the Lord had entrusted to me was restrained, because so few were willing to hear and respond to God's call by crying out in prayer, with remorse for our national massacre. Only repentance has the power to save us from reaping the grave harvest our national sin has sown.

The consequences we are facing for our failure to diligently seek God concerning this life-and-death issue are terrifying. As multiple millions were slaughtered, God reluctantly withdrew as we forfeited the divine favor that had graced America from the time of our nation's founding. In spiritual blindness we continue to empower our enemies as we ignore the only remedy that can heal us from abortion's vicious curse. That miraculous medicine is repentance and prayer.

The excruciating tragedy of 9/11 should have been an emergency wakeup call to the slumbering American church. Tragically, most believers keep hitting the snooze button every time God tries to rouse them from their deep and deadly spiritual slumber. Even though God called me to proclaim this message to American believers long ago, the sphere of my influence has been severely limited. The word of the Lord has been restrained because the church has little hunger to hear prophetic truth that calls her to awaken out of self-centered indifference and move into authentic repentance for our national atrocity.

Because we have grievously sinned by polluting our land with the shed blood of an unborn generation, God's grace of providential protection, which has hovered over America since the dawning of our nation, is slowly being withdrawn. We've seen increasing occurrences and intensification of natural disasters, such as category-four hurricanes and floods that devastate entire cities, such as New Orleans, and huge storms like Ike that leave an enormous swath of destruction in their wake. Incidents of terrorism, such as the bombing in Oklahoma City; the tragic killings of students by students at Columbine, Virginia Tech, and the University of Illinois; and the horrid events of 9/11 have also increased. These are awful, yet they are just the foreshadowing of the escalating wrath our unrepentant nation will soon incur.

America is facing a brutal harvest of death for the murderous seeds abortion has planted in the desecrated, crimson sod of our defiled land. The spirit of death and destructive events will continue to wreak havoc against the United States until the church is awakened in repentance to intercede for God's mercy. The multi-denominational church mobilized in repentance and prayer is the only genuine hope for America's deliverance. May we rise up together to seek the Lord's promise of national redemption—while there is still hope! God's grace can still triumph over judgment. This scripture should give us hope for our fallen Christian nation.

> *The instant I speak concerning a nation and concerning a kingdom, to pluck up, to pull down, and to destroy it, if that nation against whom I have spoken turns from its evil, I will relent of the disaster that I thought to bring upon it.*
>
> (Jer. 18:7–8)

Heaven's grace once shined down brightly upon us, bestowing divine favor upon "America the Beautiful." Now, instead, dark shadows of looming death and destruction hover over our guilt-ridden land. God's Word is clear. God hates the shedding of innocent blood. God's just sentence for our guilt will be executed in waves of rising terror and crushing catastrophes—unless believers are roused from their spiritual complacency and are moved to cry out in repentance for our national sin. It is time for all believers to unite in prayer to seek God for a spiritual awakening in America! We must mobilize the entire church in prayer now, before the impending wrath of God's justice consumes us!

What Is Our Mission?

The mission of *American Patriots in Prayer* is to awaken the nationwide church to the horrifying peril of escalating calamity our country is facing for the shedding of innocent blood, while we enlist believers from every denomination across America to fight for and win the lost soul of our blood-guilty nation. This can only be accomplished by saturating America with prayers of genuine repentance and fervent intercession to implore God for the cleansing of our defiled land. And we must mobilize the church in prayer quickly! *Why?*

Our entire nation is in deadly peril, because abortion has polluted America with the shed blood of an unborn generation. As silent accomplices, the indifferent church shares in the guilt for the American holocaust of the innocent unborn. In prevailing prayer or in callous complacency, it is the church alone that holds the future of the United States of America in her hands.

The mission of *American Patriots in Prayer* is being accomplished as we call believers to repentance for apathy to America's appalling sin and grave spiritual danger. Even now this message of repentance is stirring hearts to turn from inactive indifference by inspiring believers to pray for a purpose much greater than their own personal needs and desires—and much larger than their personal ambitions. Congregations are being challenged to look beyond the needs in their local church settings as they unite with other churches and denominations in the common purpose of seeking a nation-altering divine intervention. Our ministry is equipping believers through sound teaching on prayer that is based on the patterns revealed in the life of Jesus and the corporate prayer that was an effervescent wellspring and a vital foundation of church life in the first century. Apprehending the spiritual realities of New Testament Christianity that graced the early church with kingdom-advancing power is entirely possible with the under-girding of vibrant, corporate prayer.

Prayer Can Shape America's Future—Absolutely!

We can and we must experience the world-altering power that surged through first century Christianity. The twenty-first century church will be imbued with that kingdom-advancing power when frequent, fervent group prayer is embraced as an imperative foundation of church life and practice. United, praying Christians can make a genuine impact on our national destiny at this critical moment in American history through strategic, Spirit-led prayer. Opportunities are being provided as we establish a trans-denominational network of focused prayer meetings all across America, pleading for national repentance in an atmosphere of Christian unity, passionate worship, and ardent intercession. Although our vision is national in scope, the implementation is taking place heart by heart, village by village, and city by city, throughout our nation, as groups of believers unite in prayer to seek God for a spiritual awakening in our country.

Our purpose is to expose the bloodthirsty curse abortion has inflicted upon our nation by unveiling Satan's hideous threefold strategy to destroy America and bury western Christian civilization. Secondly, we are proclaiming a message of miraculous hope that clearly reveals the divine possibility of an American awakening birthed through the power of sweeping repentance and prevailing prayer. There are only two paths America can traverse: one will lead her to life and restoration; the other will plunge her to death and ruin. Either path Lady Liberty follows will bring the greatest civilization in the history of the world to her knees. Will she descend to her knees in bloody chaos at the hands of her terrifying enemies and fall to her knees from waves of cataclysmic natural disasters, or will she bow on her knees in repentance and find mercy at the foot of the blood-stained cross of Christ? In prayer or in silence, it is American believers who will determine where and how Lady Liberty will fall.

God is calling all Christian patriots to join in prayer to plead for mercy for our grievous national sins at the feet of our Blessed Redeemer. The horrifying alternative—our country falling on her knees at the feet of her savage enemies—is too awful even to contemplate.

Respect for religious conviction played no small part in the birth and early development of the United States. Thus John Dickinson, Chairman of the Committee for the Declaration of Independence, said in 1776: "Our liberties do not come from charters; for these are only the declarations of preexisting rights. They do not depend on parchments or seals; but come from the King of Kings and the Lord of all the earth." Indeed it may be asked whether the American democratic experiment would have been possible or how well it will succeed in the future, without a deeply rooted vision of divine providence over the individual and over the fate of nations.... No expression of today's commitment to liberty and justice for all can be more basic than the protection afforded to those in society who are most vulnerable. The United States of America was founded on the conviction that an inalienable right to life was a self-evident moral truth, fidelity to which was a primary criterion of social justice.

—Pope John Paul II on "The American Experiment"

For the nation and kingdom which will not serve you shall perish, and those nations shall be utterly ruined.

—Isaiah 60:12

Chapter 1

THE AMERICAN ISSUE OF BLOOD

> *And a certain woman, which had an issue of blood twelve years,*
> *and had suffered many things of many physicians, and had spent*
> *all that she had, and was nothing bettered, but rather grew*
> *worse, when she had heard of Jesus, came in the press behind,*
> *and touched his garment. For she said, If I may touch but his*
> *clothes, I shall be whole. And straightway the fountain of her*
> *blood was dried up; and she felt in her body that she was healed*
> *of that plague.*
>
> —Mark 5:25–29 (KJV)

LADY LIBERTY IS bleeding to death in the sinister clinics of malicious physicians. Her wounds are horrifying. Her hemorrhage is horrendous. She is suffering "many things of many physicians." These wicked surgeons of doom probe the sanctuary of her womb and brutally slash her offspring. They lacerate her motherhood and sever the cord that was ordained to link her to her cut-off progeny. The lethal wounds inflicting her are deeper than the natural eye could ever possibly see. The surgical weapons assaulting her are slaying the soul and assassinating the spirit of a nation.

1

The heart of America has been viciously stabbed. These slashes are appalling. The bleeding is profuse. This massacre has poured out so much blood that the savage land is utterly saturated. The heinous seepage from her barbaric slaughter has polluted her pristine rivers and turned her shining seas red with bloody guilt.

Osama Bin Laden, dead or alive, is not the issue. Radical Islam's vicious holy war is not the issue. The issue is not Iraq or Afghanistan. The Islamic fascists of Iran are not the issue. North Korea is not the issue. The aggressive resurgence of Russia is not the issue. Economic turmoil is not the issue. Weapons of mass destruction in the hands of terrorists are not the issue. These are just terrifying symptoms of our nation's mortal wound. Lady Liberty, with her damning issue of innocent shed blood—*that* is the issue!

A foul fountain of murder continually flows from Lady Liberty's violated, vacant womb. She bears a permanent wound, with a perpetual, running sore. There are no creams or ointments humankind can manufacture that would remove the deep scars that have eternally etched each of these butcheries in a book of God's remembrance. The souls of the poor innocents have not been cut off from their right to life hidden in secret. God sees every one of these murders. Heaven weeps over the tiny corpses as their dismembered bodies are wrapped in bloody rags, discarded like trash, and flushed like human waste, or incinerated like rubbish going up in hellish flames and putrid smoke. This stench in the nostrils of God has provoked Him to wrath. Appallingly, God does not have to search in secret places to find the festering gashes that are carved in cold blood as the warm blood of the innocents is ruthlessly spilled. Our national disgrace has not been veiled in grief and humiliation. It has been flaunted in arrogant haughtiness.

Our national sin has forced the reluctant withdrawal of the heavenly grace that was bestowed upon us at our nation's dawning. Through our national sin we have chosen hell's fury over God's favor. On January 22, 1973, our Supreme Court sealed a blood covenant with death that is empowering hell to destroy America. A weapon of mass destruction called *abortion* has already massacred multiple millions of innocent Americans. Because of this merciless issue of blood, America is wobbling on the brink of a terrifying plummet. God is the Sovereign King over all creation. By His decree nations rise and fall. If the church does not lead the nation into repentance, America will fall and experience the fury of God's wrath. If the church turns toward God in prevailing prayer, there is hope that America will turn from its evil and God will relent from the disastrous judgments our nation will soon incur.

> *The instant I speak concerning a nation and concerning a kingdom, to pluck up, to pull down, and to destroy it, if that nation against whom I have spoken turns from its evil, I will relent of the disaster that I thought to bring upon it.*
> (Jer. 18:7–8)

God made His requirements clear thousands of years ago when He spoke to Noah, and nowhere in Scripture does He change this dictum:

> *"Surely for your lifeblood I will demand a reckoning; . . . From the hand of every man's brother I will require the life of man. Whoever sheds man's blood, by man his blood shall be shed; for in the image of God He made man."*
> (Gen. 9:5–6)

If Lady Liberty does not get up and press into Jesus with deep repentance for her torrential hemorrhage, her reign of leadership in the world will cease. Without far-reaching repentance, mass destruction will devour millions of her citizens, crush her dreams and aspirations, crumble her infrastructure, and incinerate her wealth. Unless God's people unite in repentance and intercession, Lady Liberty does not have a prayer of being healed from the curse of her bleeding womb. The consequences from this blight of butchery in our land will progressively worsen until the famine of kingdom-advancing prayer ends in God's indifferent church. Perpetuating the plague of prayerlessness that has enfeebled multitudes in the national church would abort America's only hope, and seal the ominous reckoning our national sin has sown. Speaking through the prophet Jeremiah, God said,

> *"Has a nation changed its gods, which are not gods? But My people have changed their Glory for what does not profit. Be astonished, O heavens, at this, and be horribly afraid; be very desolate," says the LORD.*
>
> (Jer. 2:11–12)

If the heavens are astonished, how in God's name can the church on earth be so callous and apathetic? We should be astonished that America rejected her Christian heritage and abandoned the blood covenant of the Crucified Redeemer. It is more than astonishing; it is almost beyond belief! How far Lady Liberty has fallen from the grace that conferred divine favor upon her! For four damning decades, one nation under God has carved in crimson over fifty million times a cursed covenant with hell. As we sacrificed our own flesh and blood, we enthroned the very same things that Christ's death, burial, and resurrection conquered—death, hell, and the grave.

The heavens are astonished by a once God-fearing nation that now blindly worships devils. We butcher multiple millions of unborn children as offerings to Satan on scarlet-stained surgical altars. This sadistic sacrament, sealed in innocent shed blood, has crowned Satan as the new god of America! The spirit of death is now sovereign in one nation under God! Death, hell, and the grave have reigned over God's sacred gift of life for a generation!

The helpless victims of this brutality have been ripped from the hallowed sanctuary of their mother's wombs. Unless we repent for our national slaughter, oppression will abort our liberty, and the fight for our very survival will terminate our pursuit of happiness. We are on the verge of having the American dream ripped from us in a nightmare of terror and destruction.

"'Be astonished, O heavens, at this, and be horribly afraid; be very desolate,' says the LORD" (Jer. 2:12). Like the heavens, we who dwell on earth should be astonished and horribly afraid! Instead, we are apathetic and horribly complacent! This verse decrees that the nation that forsakes God will be very desolate. Still, for most professing believers, it is church as usual. Have we lost the knowledge that God is the sovereign King over all creation? Have we forgotten that God judges the nations? Where, in God's name, is the fear of the Lord in the churches of America?

> *"Because they hated knowledge and did not choose the fear of the LORD, they would have none of my counsel and despised my every rebuke. Therefore they shall eat the fruit of their own way, and be filled to the full with their own fancies. For the turning away of the simple will slay them, and the complacency of fools will destroy them."*
>
> (Prov. 1:29–32)

God forbid that we eat the fruit of our own ways! The terrifying harvest that is growing out of abortion's murderous root will eventually slay us! If we act like simpletons and do not repent and choose the fear of the Lord, the complacency of fools will destroy us! "'Be astonished, O heavens, at this, and be horribly afraid; be very desolate,' says the LORD."

The heavens are astonished because the complacent church foolishly neglected the advancement of the kingdom of God as multitudes of American believers relinquished their responsibilities as soldiers of the cross. Angels gazed in bewilderment as the church stood idly by in prayerless silence as unborn multitudes wailed in agony under a savage scalpel. The heavens were astonished as Satan ascended as the new god of choice in America on the bloody throne of sacrificial slaughter that our Supreme Court erected for him. Out of abortion's deadly roots the venomous fruit of terrorism has grown. As America massacred a generation ripped from their mothers' wombs, radical Islam infected a vicious, violent generation with pure, unrestrained hatred for America.

It is astonishing, but fifty million of our children are dead, while these satanic missionaries are grown, militant, and obsessed with suicidal zeal. They are poisoned and poised and frothing at the mouth to die as martyrs as they rip apart American civilization. The terrorism we are now beginning to reap is from the deadly terror we have sown. America needs to wake up! Abortion is terrorism against the most vulnerable members of our society! Only national repentance for our mortal sin of murdering the innocent unborn will lead us to victory in our war against the other terrorists. As long as our atrocious, surgical weapons terrorize unborn children in the hallowed haven of their mother's wombs, the curse of terrorism will plague our guilty nation.

How, in God's name, did we as a nation reject the Lord of life and through the abomination of abortion enthrone the prince of death? It is astonishing! Absolutely astonishing! However, in light of our fall from heaven's glorious grace into hell's ghastly grip, we should not be astonished that the prince of death has begun his lethal reign of terror.

The psalmist wrote, "The wicked shall be turned into hell, and all the nations that forget God" (Ps. 9:17). Our wicked slaughter is the irrefutable, damning evidence that America has forgotten God. Our nation is standing at the threshold of sweeping repentance or a descent into hellish tribulation. May the God of heaven bestow His astonishing mercy on us all!

In the light of God's favor, which our forefathers invoked and received at our nation's founding, and our providential ascent above every other civilization in the history of the world, our nation's plummet into the hellish, black darkness surpasses the depravity of Sodom and exceeds the wickedness of Gomorrah!

And you, Capernaum, who are exalted to heaven, will be brought down to Hades; for if the mighty works which were done in you had been done in Sodom, it would have remained until this day. But I say to you that it shall be more tolerable for the land of Sodom in the day of judgment than for you.

(Matt. 11:23–24)

God forbid that we receive the same just judgment of obliteration from the face of the earth!

There Still Is Hope

Will the following Scriptural promises of restoration be built on the ruins of twenty-first century America?

And they shall rebuild the old ruins, they shall raise up the former desolations, and they shall repair the ruined cities, the desolations of many generations.

(Isa. 61:4)

Yes, all kings shall fall down before Him; all nations shall serve Him.

(Ps. 72:11)

Will godliness have to rise up out of the rubble of our crushed civilization in a distant generation to fulfill these glorious prophecies? Or will the church across America fall on her knees right now and begin that restoration by rebuilding the fallen altars of persevering prayer? Will Christians unite in selfless intercession to kindle the flames of an American awakening?

Will the shedding of tears and the travail of repentance revive the church and ignite a cultural reformation? Will the twenty-first century church recover the kingdom-advancing power of unified prayer revealed in the book of Acts? Will our churches become houses of prayer, where multitudes gather to invoke heaven's miraculous intervention? Will the truth set us free and immunize our souls from the devouring plague of me-first spirituality that has coddled believers in complacency and crippled God's church in cultural impotence? Will an army of Christians in this generation get up from their beds of spiritual ease, lay down their lives, pick up the cross, fall on their knees, and arise in God's power? Will we, or will we not, restore America's godly heritage and rebuild our nation's eroded biblical foundations?

Only sweeping repentance can save us from the dreadful tsunami of wrath that is rushing toward the blood-sodden shores of our guilty nation. Will we be swept away in a furious wave of rising terror? Will our battered Christian foundations completely collapse as our political and financial institutions crumble? Will chaos prevail as the ominous swell sweeps away multitudes, pummels our cities, destroys our infrastructure, and devours our wealth? What cataclysmic event must we endure before Christians in America awaken? Will we remain in deadly denial and spiritual apathy until the darkness falls on the black night of our grim reckoning? Will we all have to endure earth-shattering judgment, death, and destruction at the hands of brutal terrorists before the church repents and unites in intercession for a spiritual awakening in our reprobate land? Will Lady Liberty fall into generations of desolation as the American church plummets into a new dark age? Will our cities be ruined in judgment while western Christian civilization is reduced to religious rubble? Will we refuse the refuge of redeeming grace and incur a plague of devouring wrath instead?

May almighty God forbid! Church of God, in the name of Jesus, unite in prayer and fight for the lost soul of our wayward country! Rebuild the altars of intercession in our houses of worship, and restore the godly foundations of American civilization! Only a national spiritual awakening will suffice! And nothing but God's people united on their knees can obtain it!

If the church at large remains entrenched in prayerless indifference, the consequences the United States will face for the curse of her bleeding womb will be devastating. Lady Liberty will fall on her knees in deep repentance for her sin of the bloody scalpel, or she will be forced to her knees by a bloody sword of savage vengeance. The Spirit of God is pleading with every Christian leader and every believer in America.

Blow the trumpet in Zion, Consecrate a fast, Call a sacred assembly; Gather the people, Sanctify the congregation, Assemble the elders, Gather the children and nursing babes; Let the bridegroom go out from his chamber, And the bride from her dressing room. Let the priests, who minister to the LORD, Weep between the porch and the altar; Let them say, "Spare Your people, O LORD, And do not give Your heritage to reproach, That the nations should rule over them. Why should they say among the peoples, 'Where is their God?'" Then the LORD will be zealous for His land, And pity His people.
(Joel 2:15–18)

The time is drawing near when Lady Liberty will fall on her knees for the abomination of abortion. Will she bow in humility and repentance, leading to life? Or will she be brutally broken in humiliation for these atrocious deaths? Where Lady Liberty will fall is a question only the church has the power to answer. However, there is no question that the greatest nation in the history of the world will soon fall on her knees.

God, grant us repentance! May we fall on our knees at Your feet and find mercy!

There are a thousand hacking at the branches of evil to one who is striking at the root.

—Henry David Thoreau

Every great movement of God can be traced to a kneeling figure.

—D. L. Moody

History belongs to the intercessors—those who believe and pray the future into being.

—Walter Wink

Chapter 2

THE FRAILTY OF CARNAL WEAPONS

If My people who are called by My name will humble themselves, and pray and seek My face, and turn from their wicked ways, then I will hear from heaven, and will forgive their sin and heal their land.

—2 Chronicles 7:14

CHRISTIAN POLITICAL ACTIVISTS have worked tirelessly for decades promoting a political right-to-life agenda. They have righteous goals and honorable motives. Regrettably, without the national church united in fervent prayer, they campaign for their cause in the political arena with the frail, carnal weapons of right-wing strategies. Are God's people completely unaware that we are in an all-out supernatural war of the greatest magnitude since Calvary? The apostle Paul wrote, "For though we walk in the flesh, we do not war after the flesh: (for the weapons of our warfare are not carnal, but mighty through God to the pulling down of strongholds)" (2 Cor. 10:3–4 KJV).

Without God's intervention in response to the national church uniting in repentance and prayer, political efforts to change the system from within the system are like trying to

11

extinguish hell's inferno with a squirt gun in one hand while attempting to catch nuclear bombs with a butterfly net held in the other. The battles pro-life activists are winning might deliver the White House, the Senate, and the House of Representatives into the hands of pro-life politicians. Yet, as great as political victories that strengthen the pro-life movement are, they cannot obtain God's grace to deliver us from the consequences our country is facing for shedding the innocent blood of more than fifty million unborn babies. This spiritual wickedness can only be uprooted by the miraculous power of the Holy Spirit. That power can only be obtained if believers unite on their knees to plead for national repentance.

Even if our Supreme Court consisted of a conservative pro-life majority that overturned *Roe v. Wade*, this, in and of itself, would not pardon America nor cancel the sentence that justice demands for our national atrocity. Deliverance from the curse this holocaust has inflicted upon our nation is impossible unless we seek and find God's grace that will grant national repentance for America's blood guiltiness. Changing our laws will not wash away the horrific crimes we have committed against innocent humanity. Fifty million times we have violated God's law which declares, "Thou shalt not kill" (Exod. 20:13 KJV). Only the prayers of the church nationwide can lead our country into repentance. Nothing less than sweeping repentance will cleanse our appalling national sin and rescind the terrifying penalty that is looming over the United States.

In no way am I implying that the church in America should be politically languorous and quietly acquiesce to the rising tide of anti-Christian bias that is rewriting history, poisoning our public education, and polluting our culture. Nor am I implying that we should hunker down and hope for the best as we hide in denial behind our flimsy stained glass windows. The church in America must aggressively engage in every facet of the political process. Yet, without the fervent prayers of the multi-faceted

American church, all other efforts are *at best* enfeebled and *at worst* completely futile.

Certainly, Christian patriots must use every legal remedy and constitutional right available to effect positive change in our government and culture. Of all of the forces at our disposal, prayer is paramount. As high as the heavens are above the earth, even so, prayer surpasses all political earthly powers. In spite of the limits inherent in our human frailty, prayer partners us with the limitless resources of the divine. Prayer and only prayer can overcome our gross national darkness and release God's redemptive light into the spiritual, cultural, and political affairs of our country.

Has the church of the living God become so spiritually numb that we actually think there could be a mere political or judicial solution that would heal our country's horrifying hemorrhage? Unfortunately, this can never be so—because America's problem is not political or judicial. Our country is inflicted with a spiritual disease that only God can heal. Our votes for pro-life politicians will not deliver Lady Liberty from the curse of her bleeding womb. All sin, even this national sin, has only one remedy. That remedy is repentance:

If My people who are called by My name will humble themselves, and pray and seek My face, and turn from their wicked ways, then I will hear from heaven, and will forgive their sin and heal their land.

(2 Chron. 7:14)

Unless the nationwide church unites in repentance and seeks God's forgiveness in prayer, all of our well-intentioned political efforts are nothing more than weak substitutes doomed to failure. At best, human efforts might slow the tide of evil, but only prayer can turn the rising tide of evil to initiate the restoration of righteousness. Our nation is at the final crossroads of revival or ruin. She needs a divine awakening! Nothing else can heal her. Lady Liberty's authentic hope is God's redemptive power, not conservative political victories. Healing our land will not come by putting our trust in a religious right-wing political agenda. Only an agenda that seeks divine intervention to cleanse our land from the travesty of abortion will suffice now.

Yes, in the past four decades our political activism has won a few skirmishes. For the meager inches we have gained, we have paid an unspeakable cost. We have suffered more than fifty million casualties, with one hundred million would-be parents eternally wounded in spirit. After all of our efforts to mobilize Christians politically, death still reigns supreme as the law of the land. In the name of God, awaken, slumbering church, and unite in prayer!

Prayer Opens Heaven's Portal to the Miraculous

From oceans of human effort, not even a single droplet of divine power can ever be distilled. Prayer and only prayer can open heaven's portal into the glorious realm where God does the impossible as heaven's intervening power is released into the affairs of nations. This is the domain where God's limitless ability waits patiently to intersect with the desperate needs of broken humanity. Prayer is the God-ordained link between human need and divine intervention, which Jesus excruciatingly secured at Calvary. The urgent need of all American believers is to seek and find forgiveness for our national slaughter. Unless the blood of Jesus washes our land from this bloody curse, we will reap a deadly harvest, as God's Word clearly forewarns:

> So you shall not pollute the land where you are; for blood defiles the land, and no atonement can be made for the land, for the blood that is shed on it, except by the blood of him who shed it.
>
> (Num. 35:33)

14

According to this scripture it will take the lives of multiplied millions of Americans to appease justice for the national disgrace of abortion that has defiled our land. There is a redeeming alternative. The shed blood of Jesus can cleanse our land, atone for this sin, and save America from reaping the full fury of this imminent judgment. Nothing but sweeping repentance has the power to deliver us from this curse, which is thirsting for our own blood.

On behalf of America, we must echo the prayer of the elders:

Provide atonement, O LORD, for Your people Israel, whom You have redeemed, and do not lay innocent blood to the charge of Your people Israel. And atonement shall be provided on their behalf for the blood. So you shall put away the guilt of innocent blood from among you when you do what is right in the sight of the LORD.

(Deut. 21:8–9)

America is polluted in innocent blood! Any authentic hope of the spiritual restoration of America is way beyond the reach of our frail human efforts and our feeble political strategies. Only a spiritual awakening birthed through prayer will suffice. Will you join us in the conquering spiritual activism of world-altering prayer? Nothing less than national repentance is adequate, and nothing less than the future of America is at stake. Child of God, humble yourself, fall on your knees, and pray!

Almighty God, provide atonement for us and grant the United States of America national repentance.

We need a baptism of clear seeing. We desperately need seers who can see through the mist—Christian leaders with prophetic vision. Unless they come soon, it will be too late for this generation. And if they do come, we will no doubt crucify a few of them in the name of our worldly orthodoxy.

—A. W. Tozer

There are no crown-wearers in heaven who were not cross-bearers here below.

—Charles Spurgeon

Chapter 3

LIFE MORE ABUNDANTLY AND THE CROSS OF CHRIST

The thief cometh not, but for to steal, and to kill, and to destroy: I am come that they might have life, and that they might have it more abundantly.

—John 10:10 (KJV)

And He said to them, "Take heed and beware of covetousness, for one's life does not consist in the abundance of the things he possesses."

—Luke 12:15

IN ETERNITY PAST, God ordained that the church would arise in the power of His life more abundantly to overcome the works of darkness and to disciple the nations. Jesus left this final command to His disciples:

Go therefore and make disciples of all the nations, baptizing them in the name of the Father and of the Son and of the Holy Spirit, teaching them to observe all things that I have commanded you; and lo, I am with you always, even to the end of the age.

(Matt. 28:19–20)

When Jesus became a man, the human and the divine were eternally, inseparably linked. We are the body of Christ in the world. We are His representatives on the earth. The redemptive work of world evangelism and the heavenly calling to disciple the nations that God has entrusted to His church are linked to our prayerful obedience. Shunning our kingdom responsibilities, while ignoring the reality of spiritual conflict with the powers of hell, does not change the fact that the powers of darkness exist. Hell is waging an all-out war against the church to foil the purpose of God in our generation. Decades of spiritual indifference by multitudes of believers in the American church have progressively surrendered one nation under God into the hideous clutch of hell.

Make no mistake about this: Satan is real. He is working feverishly to steal, to kill, and to destroy. Hell itself is conducting an unrelenting offensive against God's continuing strategy for the redemption of humankind. At the same time, God in heaven has entrusted the furtherance of the gospel to His church on earth. God has given to His people the authority to confront and the power to defeat the works of darkness.

"For we do not wrestle against flesh and blood, but against principalities, against powers, against the rulers of the darkness of this age, against spiritual hosts of wickedness in the heavenly places."

(Eph. 6:12)

Lucifer's hatred of all humankind is ruthless, but his malevolence intensifies when a soul that has found salvation in Christ fervently pursues God's life more abundantly. A believer who apprehends that more abundant life becomes a viable threat to the works of darkness. While much of the American church slumbers in the impotence of inert complacency, hell's progressive strategy to steal, to kill, and to destroy has met with little legitimate spiritual resistance. God's desire to empower

His church with life more abundantly has remained unchanged from the birth of the new covenant dispensation.

The Seed of Overcoming Life

Jesus said, "I am come that they might have life, and that they might have it more abundantly." The Greek word for life in this verse is *zoe*. *Zoe* life is the life of God that dwells in the regenerated spirit. It is the eternal life imparted at the moment of a believer's new birth. It is the life that is innate in the incorruptible seed of the Word of God, implanted within us at salvation. This life has the potential to progressively transform the redeemed soul into the very image of Christ. This *zoe* life is in total contrast with *bios* life which refers to natural or physical life, tainted by sin through the fall of man. In John 10:10, Jesus said He came to give us *zoe* life, and that *zoe* life more abundantly. He is here referring to the same life, but in differing concentrations or quantities. All true believers have a measure of this transforming life. It is the wonder of wonders to experience the infusion of this life in the new birth; yet, that is just the beginning of a supernatural life that should grow in grace and mature in power. Great spiritual authority is reserved for those who pursue that life more abundantly.

The Americanized distortion of the gospel has created a church culture that encourages believers to live a decent, moral life that focuses on learning how God will enrich us personally as He blesses us individually. Consequently, meeting the needs of individuals and families seems to be the beginning and the end of pulpit ministry in too many of our houses of worship.

Certainly, God's grace to meet our needs is inexhaustible. Although this is very true, it is very far from the whole truth. This facet of God, although it is foundational and crucial to grasp, is only partial truth. Error often results from substituting fractional truth for the whole truth. When a portion of spiritual reality is preached and accepted as God's totality, it impedes our spiritual growth and handicaps our ability to fulfill our higher purpose. It is not what the average American believer has of God that is the problem. It is the enormity of what so many of us still lack that has spiritually impoverished the church. By focusing on a gospel of self-enrichment, we have neglected the sum of God's truth. Believers have remained spiritually immature, God's church has been weakened, and the powers of hell have advanced.

The sum of God's truth clearly reveals that every believer is called to go far beyond the prevailing church culture of living in the blessings of comfortable Christianity. We are called to walk intimately with Jesus in order to experience a dynamic, kingdom-advancing spiritual life. "I am come that they might have life, and that they might have it more abundantly." Every child of God has been given life, but it grieves the Holy Spirit when we fail to pursue God in order to cultivate that life more abundantly. An abundant life is a greater portion of that very same life we received at the moment of our spiritual birth. Someone may have one hundred thousand dollars, while someone else has one hundred million. They both have money. Both have a measure of financial prosperity, but one of them has some money, while the other has material riches more abundantly and is wealthy beyond comprehension. In the same way, all Christians have God's life, but not many have matured into God's life more abundantly. Rather, they have focused on possessing an abundance of lesser "things." But, as Jesus said, "Take heed and beware of covetousness, for one's life does not consist in the abundance of the things he possesses" (Luke 12:15).

The prevailing culture of modern American Christianity has a measure of God's life, but this same Christian culture chokes out the growth of a life of authentic spiritual abundance. Today the popular, seeker-friendly version of Christianity emphasizes comfort and convenience. Personal enrichment is enthroned. Success is exalted, while bearing the cross of Christ is disregarded. Spiritual happiness is marketed as congregations are stirred emotionally but rarely provoked to obedience. It is unusual to hear preaching that rouses the hearers to surrender their all in a quest to find and fulfill the purposes of God on the earth in this generation. Personal achievement is hyped, while the role of individuals in God's ongoing redemptive purpose is very often ignored. Biblical exposition is profuse with promises of personal blessing and material prosperity. What has become nearly extinct is preaching that leads to deep, life-changing surrender that propels believers to fall on their knees in pursuit of God's highest calling. The crowds that gather in our houses of worship each Sunday are audiences to be entertained, not soldiers to be conscripted, equipped, or mobilized in prayer. Hell is at war, while the church is comfortably at rest in the perilous state of deadly denial.

Multitudes gather in church seeking a pure path that will lead to the fulfillment of their own version of the American Dream. The rugged path of self-surrender that beckons believers to bear their cross in order to pursue God's dream of humankind's redemption, spiritual awakening, and cultural reformation is incompatible with the pervasive seeker-friendly brand of American Christianity.

We instruct people how to use God rather than declaring how believers are called to become useful to Him. Instead of seeking first the kingdom of God, personal ambitions, hopes, and desires remain enthroned at the center of a lukewarm Christian experience. Jesus said, "If anyone desires to come after Me, let him deny himself, and take up his cross daily, and follow Me" (Luke 9:23). Like the world, many of the aspirations that drive believers have been shaped by our reprobate culture rather than cultivated through biblical revelation and communion with God in prayer. For God's children, there is no doubt that we have been given life, but too few of us are living in the sacred chase to apprehend that life more abundantly.

It is tragic, but much of the church world looks through the distorted lens of self to interpret spiritual things. We look for God's promise of a life of abundance to be fulfilled in personal blessings, temporal fulfillment, and the accumulation of earthly riches. Too many believers pursue this veneer of God's approval as they chase the fleeting rewards of individual goals, worldly pleasure, and material prosperity. It is a tragedy of eternal consequence when the worldly pursuit of self-satisfaction is chosen over the God-ordained path of self-surrender. Only the surrender of self enables us to enthrone Christ. This truth is absolute. To find our place in God's unfolding redemptive purpose, we must deny ourselves and pick up our cross daily. The message of the cross is in direct conflict with the prevailing gospel of self-fulfillment. When you accept one of these gospels, you automatically reject the other. Jesus is not the pure path to the American dream. If you truly follow Him as a disciple, He will lead you to Calvary, where you will lay down your life and pick up a cross of self-denial. Only by losing your life can you find His life. God's dream for each of us is that we will walk intimately with Him and find our place in His redemptive purpose. That is the essence of a more abundant life.

The True Riches of the Gospel

The greatest treasure we could ever apprehend is a life of intimacy with God that would empower us to bear eternal fruit. God, open our eyes so we can clearly see the true riches of the gospel! "Take heed, and beware of covetousness, for one's life does not consist in the abundance of the things he possesses." A life of true abundance can only be found as we live in pursuit of the true riches hidden for us in the depths of Jesus Christ. Paul's prayer for the church of the first century has become my prayer for believers living today in the twenty-first century!

That the God of our Lord Jesus Christ, the Father of glory, may give unto you the spirit of wisdom and revelation in the knowledge of him: the eyes of your understanding being enlightened; that ye may know what is the hope of his calling, and what the riches of the glory of his inheritance in the saints, and what is the exceeding greatness of his power to us-ward who believe, according to the working of his mighty power, which he wrought in Christ, when he raised him from the dead, and set him at his own right hand in the heavenly places, far above all principality, and power, and might, and dominion, and every name that is named, not only in this world, but also in that which is to come: and hath put all things under his feet, and gave him to be the head over all things to the church, which is his body, the fullness of him that filleth all in all.

(Eph. 1:17–23 KJV)

In the Americanized church, believers are enticed with crowd-gathering hype that disregards the demands of discipleship. The costly gospel of the kingdom declares that every believer is called to lay down his or her life and passionately pursue Christ in all of His fullness. God never intended that a few self-gratifying morsels would ever replace the life-transforming nourishment of His entire storehouse. Yet, rather than feasting on God's promise of a more abundant spiritual life, many believers languish in spiritual malnutrition, ingesting little more than stale, humanistic crumbs and people-pleasing religious scraps. As a result, multitudes in the church have just enough of God to be morally decent but not nearly enough to become spiritually dynamic.

With a focus on the enrichment of our individual lives, the Americanized gospel has conformed to the culture it was supposed to confront. This has created a humanistic church philosophy of *me-first* spirituality. This Christianized humanism is packaged as the pure path that will lead us to the American dream of self-enrichment. This is the same dream pursued by the ungodly.

This error in Christendom rejects the centrality of Christ and the cross by enthroning self as the object of concern and focus. In stark contrast, biblical Christianity commands us to deny ourselves by picking up our cross daily to follow in the footsteps of Jesus, Who willingly gave His life for the sake of others. The words of Jesus in this verse make the cost of discipleship very clear. "If any man will come after me, let him deny himself, and take up his cross daily, and follow me" (Luke 9:23).

God is calling the leaders of His people to confront the warped gospel of comfort and convenience that has weakened the church and left multitudes mired in lifelong spiritual infancy. Leaders must emerge with a holy boldness to proclaim God's unchanging message to this generation. We must declare the power of the cross with compassion and grace, yet without concession to the fear of man. Nothing but the preaching of the cross will mature the church and liberate believers from the errors of the modern gospel of self-fulfillment. The everlasting gospel beckons every believer to become a disciple by following Jesus on the path of self denial. A disciple finds God's life by losing his own life for the cause of Christ.

Ministers can only lead others where they are willing to go first. In these perilous times, it is imperative that Christian leaders surrender completely to the will of God. Let us walk in humility as we ask the Holy Spirit to examine our motives and purify our souls. Then we will be prepared to lead our congregations into the holy intimacy of fellowship with our heavenly Father. As God's people fulfill their high calling of lingering in God's transforming presence, they will be equipped for the humble calling of a life lived in service to others.

The Bible's richest treasures can only be discovered when we live in a passionate quest to apprehend more of God. Rather than seeking the comforts of self-fulfillment, the quest for God will always lead us to a cross of self-denial. "If anyone desires to come after Me, let him deny himself, and take up his cross daily, and follow Me." We will find the cross that Jesus beckons us to take up daily whenever, wherever, in whatever, and however our will crosses God's will. Jesus told us why He came: "I am come that they might have life, and that they might have it more abundantly." Even so, just having life is not enough to confront the intense spiritual challenges of our times. In order to pursue God's promise of an authentic, abundant life, we must surrender our will and take up our cross.

Where Are the Soldiers of the Cross?

Where are the twenty-first century soldiers of the cross? Is the church en masse so passively immersed in self-focused pursuits that she is deaf to the voice of innocent shed blood wailing? Are we too preoccupied with our personal agendas to take up our own cross and devote ourselves in prayer in order to stop this horrifying holocaust and heal this horrendous hemorrhage of human life? Are we self-absorbed to the point that we refuse to hear the weeping of the helpless, slain innocents? Have we become so biblically illiterate that we are unaware that the Scriptures reveal that shedding innocent blood will incur a grave retribution? Is our Christian faith so irrelevant that we can live our lives in superficial, spiritual happiness while the voice of innocent shed blood screams, the heart of God aches, and all of heaven weeps in astonishment over this abomination?

Where are the friends of Jesus who hear His voice, know His heart, and willingly share His burdens? Have we become so self-centered that we will let the hopes and dreams that birthed this great nation for all future generations die? Under God, Christian patriots gave birth to the United States of America. I pray to God that an army of Christian patriots will take up the cross and arise in a great movement of prayer to plead with God until America is born again. Child of God, will you become one of these patriots in prayer? I beseech you in the name of Jesus

Christ to join with us and give yourself to God in repentance and intercession. Let us fall on our knees into the merciful hands of God, before America is brought to her knees and falls into the ruthless hands of her savage enemies.

The Bible declares, "It is a fearful thing to fall into the hands of the living God" (Heb. 10:31). How much more dreadful would it be to fall out of His hands into terrifying chaos, mass destruction, and national ruin? Do not walk. Run for your life! Bow in humility and repentance at the altars of prayer! Together, on our knees, let us make God's house a house of prayer for our nation! If we continue to stagnate in the warped gospel of personal fulfillment while selfless prayer languishes in spiritual complacency, one nation under God will plummet into judgment and fade into history as the greatest fallen civilization in the history of the world! May God Almighty forbid!

"Then He said to them all, 'If anyone desires to come after Me, let him deny himself, and take up his cross daily, and follow Me'" (Luke 9:23). Child of God, deny yourself, lay down your life, take up your cross, fall on your knees, and pray!

Father, wean each of us from a frail faith that, to our shame, has often focused on little more than our own personal dreams and desires. God, give us eyes to see the great redemptive purpose that is unfolding in this generation. Spirit of God, equip our hearts to carry, in God-ordained measure, Your burden for a spiritual awakening in America and throughout the nations of the world. Deliver us from the paralyzing paradigms of self that have crippled Your church in complacency and empowered hell in ferocious fervency.

Take us beyond our limited faith that has sought Your blessing in our lives but poses little threat to the powers of darkness. Beyond the mere memorization of the words, may we possess the vibrant faith that declares, "I will 'seek first the kingdom of God, and His righteousness'" (Matt. 6:33). Grant us deep repentance for our decades of passive indifference. Forgive us for our selfish complacency that has grieved Your Holy Spirit, empowered Satan, and hindered Your redemptive purpose for the church in this nation. It was the grievous sin of our neglect that weakened Your church and enabled hell to successfully assault the godly foundations of American civilization.

As shadows of compromise crept into our divided hearts, gross darkness gripped our country. The descent of darkness eclipsed the light of our sacred history, because we who believe chose to live our lives in the dusk of self-centered spiritual mediocrity. Awaken us! We repent! We turn toward You, heavenly Father. Give us Your light and deliver us from the veil of darkness that has dimmed our spiritual eyesight.

Spirit of God, blow upon the smoldering embers in my tepid soul, and set my lukewarm heart ablaze. Cleanse me from the stench of selfishness with the precious shed blood of Jesus. May my life become a sweet-smelling sacrifice of surrender to You as I pursue You and Your kingdom purpose. As I lay my life upon the altar, may I forsake the religion of Christianized humanism that has emboldened hell and brought our nation to the brink of destruction! As I surrender my will, may I apprehend Your power through repentance and prayer. Sustain me in prayer that I might seek You fervently with the deep humility of sacrificial obedience.

Lead the American church to her ultimate purpose as our full surrender to Your providence opens heaven's portals to a renewal of our true national identity. Let Your church hear Your clarion call to fervent, united prayer. Through us, birth a twenty-first century reformation in the church and an American awakening that will ignite a cultural revolution and a worldwide heavenly visitation. Have mercy on us, and wash us from our wretched failures. In wrath, remember mercy, and grant repentance to us and to the lost multitudes in our wayward land. As we lay our lives on the altar, use our prayers to alter the eternal destinies of multiple millions across America and throughout the nations of the world. We dare to ask these things on the merits of the Blessed Redeemer of humankind alone. In boldness and faith we pray in the name of our Lord Jesus Christ.

We must, furthermore, protest the notion of manifest destiny that permits our nation to do anything it chooses. For if we insist on walking down this road, then at some point, as God is God, the God in whose eyes there is real good and real evil, we who have trampled so completely on all of God's amazing gifts to this country are going to wake up and find that He cares very much about what we do. If God exists, and if He judges good and evil, then we must realize that those who trample on His great gifts will one day know his judgment. The Scriptures bear solemn witness to this. Our nation is not immune.

—Francis Schaeffer

There is no neutral ground in the universe; every square inch, every split second, is claimed by God and counter-claimed by Satan.

—C. S. Lewis

Chapter 4

THE THREEFOLD STRATEGY OF HELL

The thief cometh not, but for to steal and to kill, and to destroy: I am come that they might have life, and that they might have it more abundantly.

—John 10:10 (KJV)

THE WORDS OF truth uttered by Jesus in John 10:10 are concise, clear, and potent. The contrast they portray is immense, and the conflict they expose is fierce. In one phrase Jesus reveals the venomous thorns of demonic strategy that hell employs to wage war against believers as devils attempt to thwart the advancement of God's kingdom. With this threefold tactic, hell endeavors to abort God's progressive, redemptive purpose entrusted to the church.

In the next phrase, Jesus expresses how a redeemed soul has the potential to ascend into authentic, godly abundance if the gift of eternal life is nurtured and cultivated into a life of spiritual maturity. It was by divine inspiration that these two thoughts were articulated in one verse. This scripture exposes Satan's three-pronged device of destruction, invented by hell to enfeeble believers, impede God's purpose, and destroy humankind. It also reveals the promise of spiritual abundance preordained in the heart of God for His

29

overcoming children. The contrast in this verse makes it clear: the destroyer's assault is ferocious, but hell is no match for believers who ascend in God to live life more abundantly.

With crushing cruelty, Lucifer tenaciously attempts to abort the high callings God has entrusted to individuals, families, churches, and even nations. Inflamed by unceasing hatred for God and malignant malice toward humankind, hell's objective is to render the church powerless in order to thwart God's unfolding redemptive purpose for humankind in every generation. "The thief cometh not, but for to steal, and to kill, and to destroy." The onslaught of hell is hot and relentless, while multitudes of American believers in this me-first generation are lukewarm and lethargic. The consequences of hell's assault against America and western Christian civilization and the spiritual passivity of the American church as a whole have been devastating and deadly.

The First Dimension of Hell's Strategy is to Steal

While multitudes of American believers settled into the complacency of comfortable Christianity, hell relentlessly besieged the foundations of our nation's godly heritage. Satan, with his threefold strategy, maliciously weakened the church while he laid the gruesome groundwork to destroy America. The pattern of demonic device revealed in John 10:10 ("The thief cometh not, but for to steal, and to kill, and to destroy") was insidiously employed as Satan and the hordes of hell systematically stole the knowledge of America's Christian heritage. The deadly propaganda of secular revisionists, who adamantly deny the reality of the Christian roots of American civilization, was concocted in hell. May almighty God stir pastors to diligently proclaim the documented facts of our country's godly legacy while they call the flocks entrusted to their care to fervent prayer!

Effectual prayer for an American awakening must include a clear understanding of the spiritual roots of our country. Our founding fathers honored and sought God in the birthing of this nation. Our God keeps His covenant even to a thousand generations. "He remembers His covenant forever, The word *which* He commanded, for a thousand generations," (Ps.105:8). The Almighty has not forgotten the living faith and believing prayers of our founders as they established this great nation on Christian principles and biblical foundations. But we, as a nation, have forsaken God, surrendered our sacred heritage, and forfeited the divine favor that was embedded at our nation's dawning.

In addition to the political documents of early American history that reflect our patriarchs' faith in God, the writings and speeches of our founders are interwoven with scriptural phrases and biblical inferences. It is a documented historical fact that more than 90 percent of those who signed the Declaration of Independence were members of Christian denominations. Many of them founded, led, or served in biblical ministries and mission endeavors. All of these historical realities reflect their dependence on the God of the Bible. Our founding fathers' deep reliance on divine providence released heaven's favor on our newborn nation.

Fervent, effectual prayer for divine intervention in our country must be based on our biblical covenants with God as believers and the historical, spiritual treasures we inherited as Christian Americans. Although America's politically correct culture denies the divine involvement that was engraved at our nation's origin, God has not forgotten the faith and prayers of the first American patriots. Even though so much of the influence and many of the symbols of our faith have been stolen from public life in America, our founders' reliance on God has not been forgotten by our heavenly Father. Even now these treasures are safely stored in the depths of God's heart. What Satan stole from us on the earth he has no access to in heaven.

The trans-denominational church of America can and must resurrect these sacred riches through prayer.

> *Who would have believed? What mind could have conceived?*
> *America, land of desolations!*
> *What has happened unto thee, the sweet Land of Liberty?*
> *The envy of all the other nations...*
> *Where's the vision that was thine when your forefathers signed,*
> *For independence, their bold Declaration?*
> *When godliness was revered, I was honored, loved, and feared.*
> *With My blessing you became a mighty nation.*

It is misplaced hope to think we can revive our godly heritage without seeking God in persevering prayer for national repentance. The devil's strategy is first to steal. After this, he kills. When he has killed, he then destroys. This pattern of demonic strategy was clearly at work when Satan stole the knowledge of the godly foundations upon which our great nation was founded. In our generation we have witnessed the erosion of our nation's fundamental belief in God, which secured the divine favor that graced the ascent of America above all other nations. With God's blessing, the United States' vibrant faith, missionary zeal, benevolence, creativity, industry, wealth, power, and influence eclipsed every other civilization in the history of the world. How far Lady Liberty has fallen from the majestic heights of heavenly favor!

How in God's name did the church allow prayer to be removed from—and then criminalized in—our schools? Where were the prevailing prayers that would have secured God's intervention as our biblically principled culture was being besieged and ravaged? The Christian moral ethic that was education's guiding light since America was founded was stolen by the demonic darkness of Darwinism, humanism, secularism, and liberalism. Where was the church while the treasures in our house were being plundered? While we slept, the devil stole the divine rudiments upon which our Republic was established under God by our Christian patriarchs. The very foundations of morality and civility contained in the Ten Commandments are being trodden under the feet of demons as they seek to remove all public symbols of faith in God in America. To our shame we have ignored the clarion warning of Jesus: "The thief cometh not, but for to steal, and to kill, and to destroy." These are not irrelevant religious words. They contain a heavenly warning that American Christians as a whole failed to heed. In the first dimension of demonic strategy, the thief comes to steal. It is tragic, but God's church did not guard the gates to our treasury. As a result, the first dimension of hell's strategy was accomplished as the thief stole our national spiritual riches.

The Second Dimension of Hell's Strategy is to Kill

Until the devil weakened the church and stole the Christian morality that was intricately woven throughout the fabric of American society, he could not enter the second dimension of his malignant purpose, to kill. The climax of our spiritual neglect, which had paved the way for the drug-induced sexual revolution of the 1960s, was fully manifested when abortion was legalized in America. *Roe v. Wade* is our nation's cursed legal document that sanctioned hell to enter the second dimension of Satan's strategy to destroy America. That second dimension is to kill. Make no mistake about this: Satan is a murderer. He is the malignant mastermind behind abortion. Fifty million helpless, innocent babies have been wickedly murdered in our nation. Hell rejoiced while we viciously executed an innocent generation, ripped from the sacred sanctuary of their mothers' wombs.

This holocaust is an outrage against God and nature. In light of our sacred heritage, the depth and breadth of our savage slaughter must be the most horrific national sin in the history of the world. For four condemning decades this brutal butchery has continued unabated as the second dimension of hell's strategy—to kill—has succeeded.

Through abortion, our entire nation is wobbling on the brink of terrifying tribulation. Justice is demanding our blood be shed in retribution for our national sin. It is only our lifeblood or the life-giving blood of the Crucified Redeemer that can quench this rapacious blood thirst.

> So you shall not pollute the land where you are; for blood defiles the land, and no atonement can be made for the land, for the blood that is shed on it, except by the blood of him who shed it.
>
> (Num. 35:33)

Nothing but deep national repentance has the power to avert a catastrophic harvest of death of American citizens for the fifty million murderous seeds of death we have so viciously sown.

In spiritual blindness, through this horrendous slaughter, America's soul has been sold to the devil. Through abortion we have made a blood covenant with death and hell.

> Yea, they sacrificed their sons and their daughters unto devils, and shed innocent blood, even the blood of their sons and of their daughters, whom they sacrificed unto the idols of Canaan: and the land was polluted with blood.
>
> (Ps. 106:37–38 KJV)

The American church must awaken immediately in order to avoid an even greater catastrophic judgment than that which befell Israel for the same horrific sin they committed when they sacrificed their sons and daughters. What comparatively was a trickle of blood in ancient Israel is now a torrential Niagara that pours unceasingly from America's haunted hollow womb.

Therefore was the wrath of the LORD kindled against his people, insomuch that he abhorred his own inheritance. And he gave them into the hand of the heathen; and they that hated them ruled over them. Their enemies also oppressed them, and they were brought into subjection under their hand.

(Ps. 106:40–42 KJV)

Sweeping Repentance or Shattering Ruin

We have entered the time when America is beginning to reap the gruesome harvest her wicked massacre has sown. America is at the crossroads of sweeping repentance or shattering ruin. If we do not repent, this terrifying scripture will be fulfilled: "They that hated them ruled over them. Their enemies also oppressed them, and they were brought into subjection under their hand." As believers we must take responsibility by repenting for our national outrage. Without repentance we are all at grave risk from the bloodthirsty terrorists that abhor us with unrestrained suicidal hatred. If we turn toward God with humility and regret, the following verse can give us hope.

When Israel cried out to God in genuine repentance in the midst of her afflictions, God regarded her, remembered His covenant, and showed her mercy:

Nevertheless he regarded their affliction, when he heard their cry: and he remembered for them his covenant, and repented according to the multitude of his mercies.

(Ps. 106:44–45 KJV)

God has not forgotten the original intent and the believing prayers of America's Christian founding fathers, but their descendents forsook righteousness and drifted away from God. As godliness waned in America, our Christian heritage eroded until the Lord of life was completely and officially rejected by the highest judicial authority in our land. In blind judgment, the spirit of death was exalted over life and enthroned to reign when our Supreme Court made our blood covenant with hell called *Roe v. Wade*. For four damning decades we have walked in the gory bondage of that hellish covenant. Daily that cursed covenant is renewed in fresh blood as we sacrifice our own sons and daughters unto devils in cold-blooded murder on surgical altars. *Where, in God's Name, are the prevailing prayers of God's people?*

Abortion is the ultimate idolatry and the vilest form of unrestrained, satanic worship. This legal contract between the United States and Lucifer has been savagely sealed with the lifeblood of our children. Without repentance, the reign of death in America will soon spread beyond the unborn multitudes like a devouring plague across our guilty land. Only deep, national repentance will revoke America's blood covenant with hell, release us from Satan's reign of tyranny, and restore divine favor to our nation. Abortion completely fulfilled the second dimension of hell's malicious strategy, to kill. Our wicked massacre has brought American civilization to the threshold of the third dimension of hell's hideous plan, to destroy.

The Third Dimension of Hell's Strategy is to Destroy

Hell rejoiced in the killing of multiple millions as the second dimension of Satan's strategy to destroy America was completed. Multitudes were led to the slaughter, because so few of God's people apprehended the power of God's life more abundantly to confront and conquer this debilitating curse. Our criminal complacency empowered hell as devils pillaged our spiritual treasures in the first dimension, which is to steal. Then, hell incited the massacre of a helpless generation in the second dimension, which is to kill. Rather than national revival birthed through God's church humbly uniting in the power of overcoming prayer, God's people insulated themselves from reality in deadly denial and spiritual indifference. While we focused on a faith of personal enrichment, with little emphasis on our spiritual responsibilities for the advancement of God's kingdom, a godless, self-centered, vile, and pornographic culture of death and violence insidiously permeated every facet of American society. As the church retreated, hell advanced and heaven wept.

While the pampered church embraced a gospel of self-fulfillment, hell's malicious purpose progressed nearly unchallenged through the first two stages of its threefold strategy to destroy America. The massive carnage of the helpless innocents reveals the terrifying truth that hell's three-dimensional plan to destroy American civilization is succeeding—because it has met so little spiritual resistance from the majority of God's people. We who are true believers do have God's life, but too few of us are seeking to apprehend that life more abundantly. The consequences we are on the verge of reaping for the apathetic spiritual lives we have sown are horrific. The church world's lethal lethargy is shamefully mirrored in the murders of unborn multitudes. The spiritual impotence of many of God's children has hindered heaven's purpose in the earth and emboldened hell, while demons continue to execute Lucifer's three-pronged attack. Our spiritual negligence empowered hell to steal a godly national heritage and to kill a generation of unborn children. Our damning bloodguilt is now empowering hell to enter the third satanic dimension, which is to destroy.

We are now beginning to see this third terrifying level of demonic strategy as hell's ultimate purpose for our guilt-ridden nation unfolds. The brutal acts of terrorism we have endured were just the beginnings of hell's escalating war to exterminate Christian society and devastate a reprobate America. The world-wide jihad of murderous religious fanatics, the Islamic Nazis of Iran—hell-bent to kill Christian infidels while wiping Israel off the face of the earth—the nuclear ambitions of demented dictators, the rabid pursuit of weapons of mass destruction by insane terrorists are all part of hell's continuing strategy to destroy western Christian civilization.

The powers of darkness are warring against the church to annihilate what little remains of the Christian foundations in American society. Nothing less than deep repentance and the mobilization of the church in America, with all of her spiritual resources, are capable of stopping this demonic onslaught. Hell was able *to steal* our nation's Christian foundations. Our Supreme Court empowered hell *to kill* an unborn generation. Our wicked slaughter has brought America under judgment that is empowering hell *to destroy* our nation. If we do not repent now, our sin of prayerless indifference will abort God's purpose for the twenty-first century church in America!

In light of the horrifying terror we have sown, we are without authentic hope of averting a catastrophic reaping, unless multitudes arise in the church determined to pursue and apprehend the powers of life more abundantly. That pursuit would lead the church at large back to God on her knees in repentance and prayer. Nothing else will secure God's mercy to cleanse us from our appalling bloodguilt. Only the power of national repentance is capable of finding the grace of redemption from our loathsome national sin. Nothing less than national repentance can save America from the forces of hell that are destroying our country. "The thief cometh not, but for to steal, and to kill, and to destroy."

A Hidden War

The devil stole our godly American heritage as he pilfered our Christian moral foundations. Then, as we murdered an innocent generation, our national atrocity slashed the heart and butchered the soul of one nation under God. This life-or-death conflict will be recorded in the eternal annals of history as this nation's spiritual civil war. We must war against the powers of hell itself, which are seeking to totally destroy not only our Christian foundations but also our entire civilization. There is no political, law enforcement, or military power capable of winning this very real, underlying, spiritual warfare. America will either fall in defeat and desolation or in national repentance rise in victory to restoration.

The outcome of this hidden war raging in heavenly places has been beyond the grasp of most of our religious and political leaders. It is self-evident that it was not comprehended by a majority of those who wear the scarlet-stained robes in the darkened chambers of our reprobate Supreme Court. It was in that court where America's soul was sold to the devil when our blind justices made America's blood covenant with death a generation ago. The outcome of this conflict between life and America's blood covenant with hell will determine our nation's ultimate fate in the twenty-first century: repentance or ruin. America the Beautiful has now begun to reap nothing more than the destruction she has recklessly and viciously sown. For four decades, the voice of innocent blood has unceasingly cried up from the ground into the ears of God, who created man in His very own image. From sea to shining sea, the land of the Pilgrims' pride is now shamefully polluted in bloody guilt. Even as the blight of slavery ripened into a horrific civil war, a plague of death is looming.

By the sweat of the slaves' brows were your cotton fields all plowed.
Like oxen, herded onto your plantations.
By the slaves that you owned, were the seeds of Civil War sown,
As they cried out to Me in desperation.
They shed blood, sweat, and tears by your injustices for years,
Till I arose in my indignation.
I smote your land with the sword, for this brutality I abhorred.
With your blood I brought Emancipation.

Nationally, we have forsaken the God of our founding fathers and enthroned death to reign by rejecting the Lord of life and His eternal command: "Thou shalt not kill" (Exod. 20:13 KJV). We have brought our entire nation under the curse that Cain incurred when he slew his righteous brother Abel.

What hast thou done? The voice of thy brother's blood crieth unto me from the ground. And now art thou cursed from the earth, which hath opened her mouth to receive thy brother's blood from thy hand.

(Gen. 4:10–11 KJV)

God hears the wailing of the innocent blood of the unborn as the slain multitudes cry up in sorrow from the ground.

Up from the ground I again hear the sound
Of innocent blood being shed in your nation.
It's the cry of the unborn, from their mothers' wombs they're torn,
As they gasp for life in desperation.
What is this that thou hast done?
They're your daughters. They're your sons.
My greatest gift—the crown of My creation.
I am girding on My sword. These ruthless murders I abhor.
I will smite again your blood-guilty nation.

The Righteous Judge of the whole earth would no longer be the God of life, love, and justice if He ignored their wailing by allowing our heinous sin to go unpunished and our national atrocity to fester forever in the bleeding womb of what was once a God-fearing nation. Our country is under the curse of Cain, because all across America, innocent shed blood cries up from the ground into the ears of God. Because of this bloody curse, America will never again have lasting peace, security, and prosperity—until she repents of this abomination and a constitutional amendment forever enthrones an unborn child's right to life in one nation under God. America is at a critical juncture that will lead her to national repentance or plunge her into decades of destruction. If we refuse to repent and continue to harden our hearts, America will fall into calamitous ruin and devastating disarray at the hands of her savage adversaries and by the fury of intensifying natural disasters.

We legalized the murder of the unborn, and fifty million innocent children were ruthlessly slaughtered. Our entire country is contaminated in this plague of gory condemnation. Empowered by our wicked massacre, hell is ascending in terror to utterly decimate America. The eternal destinies of multiple millions of lost souls and the entire population of our country are in deadly peril. First Satan steals. Then he kills. Ultimately, he destroys. God is weeping over the prayerlessness of His people. In the name of God, I implore you to awaken and fall on your knees.

Why are my people still asleep? I behold you and I weep.
The only hope of your dying nation!
Unaware of gathering gloom, apart from you, America's doomed.
Church of God, where is your consecration?
By your pleasures you're still bound. On your knees you're rarely found,
Crying out with tears and supplications.
For her sins My fury's stored. By the church, I'm still ignored.
Shall I come in wrath, or restoration?

A mediocre spiritual life is completely inadequate at this destiny-determining moment of American history. God's only answer to hell's vicious offensive has remained unchanged from the moment two thousand years ago when these words left the lips of Jesus: "I am come that they might have life, and that they might have it more abundantly." In the name of Jesus, child of God, choose life...His abundant life. *Fall on your knees and pray!*

The physician who should pamper a man in his disease, who should feed his cancer, or inject continual poison into the system, while at the same time he promised sound health and long life—such a physician would not be one half so hideous a monster of cruelty as the professed minister of Christ who should bid his people take comfort, when, instead thereof, he ought to be crying, "Woe unto those that are at ease in Zion: be troubled, you careless ones."

—Charles Spurgeon

A dense black cloud was coming up behind us.... You could hear the shrieks of women, the wailing of infants, and the shouting of men....People bewailed their own fate or that of their relatives, and there were some who prayed for death in their terror of dying. Many besought the aid of the gods, but still more imagined that there were no gods left, and that the universe was plunged into eternal darkness forevermore.

—Pliny, on the eruption of Vesuvius, A.D. 79

Chapter 5

DEADLY DENIAL

*Son of man, speak to the children of your people, and say to them:
"When I bring the sword upon a land, and the people of the land
take a man from their territory and make him their watchman,
when he sees the sword coming upon the land, if he blows the
trumpet and warns the people, then whoever hears the sound of
the trumpet and does not take warning, if the sword comes and
takes him away, his blood shall be on his own head. He heard the
sound of the trumpet, but did not take warning; his blood shall be
upon himself. But he who takes warning will save his life. But if the
watchman sees the sword coming and does not blow the trumpet,
and the people are not warned, and the sword comes and takes any
person from among them, he is taken away in his iniquity; but his
blood I will require at the watchman's hand." So you, son of man:
I have made you a watchman for the house of Israel; therefore you
shall hear a word from My mouth and warn them for Me.*

—Ezekiel 33:2–7

THE THREAT OF the rumbling volcano was seen for
hundreds of miles as she belched acrid smoke and spewed
suffocating ash. Releasing but a wisp of her deep-seething
anger darkened a cloudless blue sky and polluted the pristine
mountain air. Washington State authorities raced to evacuate

tourists and residents as the scientific community asserted to all who would listen that the writhing mountain could erupt at any moment.

Sirens blared the shrill forewarning that the fury of the volcano might soon be released in an explosive river of molten lava, destroying everything in its path. Families fled from the impending danger in fear of their lives. Leaving their homes and dreams, they ran with little more than their memories, forsaking possessions in a rush to escape to safety. The swift exodus saved almost everyone from the furious wrath of the fuming volcano.

Harry Truman was not one of them. He was caretaker of a lodge on Spirit Lake, five miles north of the boisterous, smoldering peak. Harry felt the incessant rumbling of the enraged mountain. He coughed from the sulfurous smoke and gagged on the choking ash. He heard all of the warnings, looking on as the guests at his lodge joined the hurried flight of frightened families downhill to safety. He ignored the pleas of his vacating visitors and refused to follow his fleeing coworkers or join his escaping neighbors. Entrenched in fatal obstinacy, he refused to leave, even when his sister phoned, begging him to go. I can still remember Harry smiling on national television declaring proudly, "Nobody knows more about this mountain than Harry. It don't dare blow up on him."

On May 18, 1980, at 8:32 A.M., Mount Saint Helens exploded. In seconds, everything was completely obliterated for 150 square miles. Harry, the lodge, and Spirit Lake were instantaneously entombed in fifty feet of mud, rock, and volcanic ash. That devastating eruption at Mount Saint Helens released a force 500 times greater than the nuclear bomb that leveled Hiroshima. Harry should have heeded the warnings.

Apocalyptic Rumblings

There is a smothering indifference in the American church to the grave danger looming in the hellish darkness that hovers over the United States. While the tranquilized church contentedly sleeps unaware, a terrifying national calamity could erupt at any moment with hell's putrefying fury. Are the caretakers of His American flock oblivious to the fact that our nation is perched on a rumbling peak, poised to explode in cataclysmic devastation? If they are asleep, someone needs to sound God's shrill siren to immediately arouse them. If His shepherds are awake, then how in God's name can they remain silent as His sheep naively graze on a writhing mountain doomed to explode?

Is it possible that, like Harry, the caretakers of God's people are in deadly denial of the grave peril of impending retribution for our grievous national sin? Has our reprobate culture inoculated them from the eternal truth that shedding innocent blood will sow a sure recompense of shed blood which, apart from repentance, must be reaped? After four bloody decades, has abortion fatigue plummeted pastors into a deceptive spiritual coma that justifies their lukewarm spirits as they silently acquiesce to the murder of the innocent unborn?

How has this lethal rejection of reality made Christian leaders oblivious to America's imminent danger for her heinous sin? Don't they hear the terrifying rumblings that warn of the approaching day of her apocalyptic retribution? The air is polluted with sulfurous ash. Can't they smell the odious stench of hell's putrid belching, which is threatening to erupt in deadly terror? Where are the prophets of God—those who will arise courageously in the name of God to shake these apathetic leaders until they awaken and repent from their cruel indifference?

Our National Accountability

On our watch fifty million unborn children have been led to slaughter. Are American pastors, who are so biblically educated, unaware that this holocaust has brought our entire nation under a condemning curse of bloody guilt? Our land is polluted in innocent, shed blood, and God is not silent regarding the consequences for our national abomination:

So you shall not pollute the land where you are; for blood defiles the land, and no atonement can be made for the land, for the blood that is shed on it, except by the blood of him who shed it.

(Num. 35:33)

This terrifying scripture alone should be more than enough to provoke all of God's leaders to call the church across America to repentance and prevailing prayer. Our national sin of shedding innocent blood has left a grave debt that must be paid in full. That debt of shed blood can only be repaid in shed blood. The cold-blooded murder of fifty million unborn children has put the entire population of the United States at deadly risk. Apart from deep national repentance, this bloodthirsty curse will eventually decimate the population of the United States and devastate American civilization as we know it.

The preoccupied church is not guiltless, and believers will not find a way of escape without leading the entire nation into repentance.

Also in thy skirts is found the blood of the souls of the poor innocents: I have not found it by secret search, but upon all these. Yet thou sayest, Because I am innocent, surely His anger shall turn from me. Behold I will plead with thee, because thou sayest, I have not sinned.

(Jer. 2:34–35 KJV)

The scarlet stains of innocent shed blood have soaked America's skirts. Her filthy rags are sodden with the issue of blood that pours continuously from Lady Liberty's haunted, hollow womb. This blood has also splattered on the pious, religious garb worn by multitudes of professing believers who say, "I am innocent; surely His anger will turn from me."

Criminal Complacency

When *Roe v. Wade* legalized the murder of the unborn, American Christians should have agonized in unrelenting prayer, imploring heaven for divine intervention. Our complacency was criminal. The church nationwide should have united in prevailing prayer against this national abomination until abortion in America was abolished. With holy outrage, the trans-denominational church should have been unified and mobilized in repentance for our national sin, interceding for the lives of the poor innocents and praying for our nation's return to moral and judicial sanity. Instead, we chose the feeble weapons of politics and protest over prayer and penitence.

Neglecting God's remedy, we sowed the frail power of political activism and reaped the murders of fifty million unborn children. Where politics failed, our united, fervent prayers would have prevailed. While Ronald Reagan stood as one rare exception, many leaders on the right engaged in pro-life political posturing to win votes, but once they were elected they avoided engaging in real pro-life battles to win this war on human life itself. Many of these conservative politicians have done little more than appease the pro-life Christian right.

Will we ever learn that political activism is a weak substitute for the limitless power of God that can only be obtained through fervent prayer? Political activism is noble and our votes have value, but only prayer can cross the threshold into the miraculous. Nothing but prayer is capable of empowering our efforts in the battle between life and our vile culture of death. The Christian right organized politically, but the church at large neglected to assemble in kingdom-advancing, nation-altering prayer. Hence the carnage of unborn multitudes continues unabated, and our nation is wobbling at the very brink of terrifying judgment.

The deadly wounds abortion has inflicted on our nation are not political or judicial; they are spiritual. No messianic candidate will ever be elected who will have the power to heal our mortal national wound. There are no congressional fixes, governmental remedies, or political pharmaceuticals to treat the malignant guilt our nation bears for slaughtering fifty million innocent unborn children. The heavenly medicines of repentance and prayer are the only possible cures that can heal Lady Liberty from the bloodthirsty curse of her bleeding womb.

Father, Forgive Us

Though we mobilized believers in politics and protests, when we neglected to unite the church in persevering prayer, we became the reluctant but guilty accomplices in this national holocaust. God's light is exposing the guilt of spiritual lethargy that many believers have tried to cloak in the threadbare rags of political activism. "Also in thy skirts is found the blood of the souls of the poor innocents: I have not found it by secret search, but upon all these" (Jer. 2:34). It is time to cleanse the tattered, bloodstained robes of self-righteous Christians, who neglect prayer while they arrogantly assert their innocence: "Behold I will plead with thee, because thou sayest, I have not sinned...."

How dare we say we have not sinned when God declares that we are stained with the blood of the souls of the poor innocents? Believers will not be immune from the outbreak of judgment that will spread across our defiled, unrepentant land. The frayed fabric of our society will unravel and impact every American.

Our national sin will incur national judgment unless, as a nation, we invoke heaven's mercy. There is no place to run for safety but to the feet of God—and nowhere to hide from the terrible fury of His righteous indignation.

While the four decade massacre of the unborn innocents continues to this day throughout our land, only a few of God's people are committed to stopping it with the heavenly remedy of prevailing prayer. Astoundingly, for most it has been church as usual. The indifferent church has been stained with the blood of the poor innocents. With acquiescing apathy rather than overcoming outrage, most professing believers have quietly condoned the barbaric butchery taking place in America. Still, it is not too late for grace and mercy to triumph over guilt and judgment. Our repentance must be sweeping and swift, before the full force of national judgment erupts without remedy.

God's leaders must boldly call for repentance for our atrocious guilt, while declaring the clear and present danger of an ominous national recompense. What devastating natural disaster or savage act of terrorism will it take to drive the church to her knees? Must we reap the catastrophic bloodbath we have sown before the slumbering church awakens to repent before the face of God? Will we regard the clarion call to proclaim the Bible's condemnation of the murder of the unborn, or will we continue in terminal spiritual denial, until devastation awakens us to our sin? Remember the words God spoke to Ezekiel:

> *But if the watchman sees the sword coming and does not blow the trumpet, and the people are not warned, and the sword comes and takes any person from among them, he is taken away in his iniquity; but his blood I will require at the watchman's hand.*
> (Ezek. 33:6)

God forbid that church leadership would remain silent while
every person entrusted to its care is in deadly peril! Church leaders
have a grave responsibility and an urgent duty to mobilize their
parishioners in prayer. United, on our knees, we must plead with
God for mercy until we receive forgiveness and gain heaven's
intervention. All across America pastors and congregations must
turn towards God and build altars of fervent prayer and ardent
intercession to beseech God for national repentance.

The Scriptures are clear. Our blood will be shed unless the
shed blood of the Crucified Redeemer cleanses our land from
this filthy curse of bloodthirsty guilt. United in indifference, the
continuing complacency of the church will seal the dreaded fate
of a guilt ridden nation damned in a bloody rebellion against
God and nature.

There is only one solution. The church, by humbly uniting
in a great wave of repentance and prayer, could call upon heaven
to fulfill God's infallible promise: healing obtained through
repentance. Our obedience to meet God's conditions on our
knees would release the glorious grace to forgive our sin and
attain God's astounding promise to heal our land:

> *If My people who are called by My name will humble themselves,
> and pray and seek My face, and turn from their wicked ways,
> then I will hear from heaven, and will forgive their sin and
> heal their land.*
>
> (2 Chron. 7:14)

Pastor, run for your life—along with your congregation—to
the altar of hell-shaking, world-swaying prayer! Lead your
assembly into repentance. Gather the people of God to pray
to save our country from the impending fury of hell's molten
devastation. Do it now—before hell erupts! Do it now—for
the sake of your flock, for their children, and for all future
generations of Americans. Unless the American church falls

on her knees, Lady Liberty does not have a prayer. Minister of God, I implore you in the name of Jesus, from this day forward, give her your prayers, and those of your congregation! We are all in grave peril. To continue in denial would be deadly! The silence of God's leaders is inexcusable! In God's name, I beseech you: Call your parishioners to prayer—today! Do it now before the full fury of judgment explodes and nation-altering devastation erupts!

Nonviolence means avoiding not only external physical violence but also internal violence of spirit. You not only refuse to shoot a man, but you refuse to hate him.
—Martin Luther King, Jr.

Social justice cannot be attained by violence. Violence kills what it intends to create.

—Pope John Paul II

Chapter 6

FATHER, FORGIVE THEM, FOR THEY KNOW NOT WHAT THEY DO

If My people who are called by My name will humble themselves, and pray and seek My face, and turn from their wicked ways, then I will hear from heaven, and will forgive their sin and heal their land.

—2 Chronicles 7:14

GOD'S PRESCRIPTION FOR healing our land is found above in this simple verse. It is pointed, concise, and unmistakably clear. God's people must humble themselves and pray. Prayer is the only cure for America's terminal spiritual disease. The other formulas of political activism and right-wing strategies that we have applied to the deadly wound of abortion for four decades have barely slowed the incessant bloodshed, much less cauterized Lady Liberty's ravaged womb.

The depths of America's spiritual scars are horrifying. There are no earthly medicines or political cures that can stop the bleeding and heal these festering gashes. Without the church uniting in prayer, all of our other well-intentioned but human efforts to see America healed and restored are doomed to failure. Only God has the power to heal our land from the curse we inflicted upon ourselves by shedding the innocent blood of fifty million unborn children. The butchered womb of Lady Liberty will be fatal without applying God's only remedy. We must humble ourselves in repentance and prayer. The battle for the bleeding womb, the failing heart, and the lost soul of America will never be won...unless believers from every denomination unite together to plead with God on their knees.

Our Warfare is Spiritual not Carnal

We are in a spiritual war of the greatest magnitude since Calvary. This war can only be waged and won with the weapons of prayer. The warped souls who think they are serving God as they bomb clinics, threaten their workers, or shoot abortionists will not find an ally in any American Patriots in Prayer group. Those twisted anarchists have denied the very faith they disgracefully allege they are fighting for. All of these fanatic combative people who advocate the use of physical violence in this spiritual war deserve to reap the consequences the courts are empowered to execute for their lawless behavior. Vicious acts of cruelty in the clinics of death are the problem. More violent acts or threats by extremist radicals at the offices of abortionists are not the solution.

There is a real war being waged, but it is not against abortionists and the lost souls who work in these death chambers. Attacking them will never promote life. We are in a spiritual conflict against "principalities and powers, the rulers of the darkness of this world, and spiritual wickedness in high places" for the unborn innocents, the lost soul, and the bleeding womb of our dying nation.

We are not wrestling against flesh and blood. Our battle is a spiritual one that can only be won on our knees, fighting with the spiritual weapon of prayer. Rather than hatred, threats, and more brutality, all genuine pro-life people need to bombard heaven, passionately pleading for God's mercy and forgiveness—even for the lost souls of the abortionists who these misled militants rabidly abhor. Death, hatred, and violence are the real adversaries of authentic Christianity. Our conquest of abortion and the bloody curse it has inflicted on America must begin by purging from among us all the twisted souls who outrageously claim to be fighting for life while the same spirit of hatred that spawned abortion grips their deluded hearts.

Believers are called to put on the very nature of Christ, who willingly laid down His life in love to pay the ultimate price of redemption, even for His enemies' divine deliverance. Love flowed unabated through the parched, blistered lips of Jesus as He hung dying on the bloody cross. He pled for the salvation of the savage souls of those who had viciously butchered Him there: "Father, forgive them; for they know not what they do" (Luke 23:34). Only love this deep and pure united with forgiveness this inclusive and absolute can sanction our prayers to obtain God's grace that is so undeserved but so desperately needed.

Clearly, Satan is the wicked mastermind behind America's reprehensible slaughter. Abortion is a deadly manifestation of the spirit of Lucifer, whose very nature is hatred. Hatred toward any human being has no place in the pro-life movement. The deep, twisted roots of abortion sprouted out of hatred for God and humankind in the bowels of hell itself. Hatred will never conquer hatred, but hatred always conquers those who hate. Until the church understands who the real enemy is and unites in prayer to uproot this devilish blight at its source, the spirit of hatred and death will continue the relentless massacre of the innocents.

We face a blinding, subversive, spiritual enemy that is hidden, hideous, and deviously deceptive. Only the power of love can conquer it! Thus, if the church unites in the love of Christ to give herself in fervent intercession, even for those who vehemently oppose the right to life, the Spirit of God will begin to expose the tactics of the real enemy. Then the ardent prayers of the united church across America would devastatingly enfeeble Satan, and our triumphant intercessions would utterly humiliate him. United in prevailing prayer, the church would enforce the conquest over hell that the sacrifice of Jesus at Calvary secured.

In the ravaged refuge of the vulnerable unborn, it is the Prince of Darkness who has twisted and severed the bloody cord that is now strangling America. Only a great wave of prayer leading to national repentance will save us from abortion's suffocating grip of death and deliver Lady Liberty from the curse of her bleeding womb. In God's name, I beseech you to join with us in repentance and prayer until love and life conquer hatred and death.

I want deliberately to encourage this mighty longing after God. The lack of it has brought us to our present low estate. The stiff and wooden quality about our religious lives is a result of our lack of holy desire. Complacency is a deadly foe of all spiritual growth. Acute desire must be present or there will be no manifestation of Christ to His people. He waits to be wanted. Too bad that with many of us He waits so long, so very long, in vain.

—A. W. Tozer

Love is kindled in a flame, and ardency is its life. Flame is the air which true Christian experience breathes. It feeds on fire; it can withstand anything rather than a feeble flame; but when the surrounding atmosphere is frigid or lukewarm, it dies, chilled and starved to its vitals. True prayer must be aflame.

—E. M. Bounds

Chapter 7

THE INBORN SPARK OF REDEMPTIVE INTERCESSION

"Therefore let all the house of Israel know assuredly that God has made this Jesus, whom you crucified, both Lord and Christ." Now when they heard this, they were cut to the heart, and said to Peter and the rest of the apostles, "Men and brethren, what shall we do?" Then Peter said to them, "Repent, and let every one of you be baptized in the name of Jesus Christ for the remission of sins; and you shall receive the gift of the Holy Spirit. For the promise is to you and to your children, and to all who are afar off, as many as the Lord our God will call." And with many other words he testified and exhorted them, saying, "Be saved from this perverse generation." Then those who gladly received his word were baptized; and that day about three thousand souls were added to them. And they continued steadfastly in the apostles' doctrine and fellowship, in the breaking of bread, and in prayers.

—Acts 2:36-42

THE PURE GOSPEL awakening that gushed from the pristine wellspring of the early church was birthed at the end of a ten day prayer meeting. That divine outpouring was obtained, then sustained, by a movement of prayer that never waned throughout the history of the first-century church recorded in the book of Acts.

After ten days of united prayer in an upper room in Jerusalem, the heavens were opened and God's church was empowered by the Holy Spirit to impact a fallen world with His miraculous gospel. Fresh out of the womb of Pentecost, the newborn church won the lost, healed the sick, and raised the dead. As she prayed, the gospel she lived and preached shook the entire civilized world. Through prayer, the bride of Christ rose above the rage of relentless religious adversity. It was prayer that emboldened her and empowered her as the first-century church gave birth to Christianity and altered the course of human history. Upon the apostolic foundations of community life, God graced them with kingdom advancing power. Because frequent gatherings of corporate prayer were foundational, the church lived in the radiance of God's presence and experienced the reality of His miraculous intervention.

Simple praying men and women with a profound message provoked persecution from the same religious leaders who persecuted Jesus and incited His crucifixion. The perpetual assault that was waged against them only fueled the inferno of fervent, unrelenting prayer in the blazing, infant church. Through the weapon of prayer, heaven's power triumphed over all demonic and earthly opposition. God's purpose prevailed as prayer miraculously established the bright light of the gospel in the midst of the gross spiritual darkness that reigned in an antagonistic, anti-Christian culture.

Flourishing in adversity, the onslaught of continuous external harassment only strengthened the church's commitment to advance God's kingdom through the power of prevailing prayer. Mightily empowered through time spent in God's presence, the persecuted church found spiritual strength in prayer that fortified them with unassailable inner resolve and graced them with supernatural power. The persistent demonic assaults that continually warred against them, time after time, incurred miraculous divine retribution.

Great numbers were added to the church while the believers lifted their hearts in prayer to God. Accelerated vexation of the believers through threats, beatings, stonings, and slaughter only intensified their prayer-thrust, which accelerated the pace of divine visitation. Miracles increased, and the gospel spread rapidly. In hell it became painfully evident that persecution alone would never stop this advancing kingdom. God's church was united in world-altering prayer, and hell was powerless to stop it. These prophetic words of Jesus were becoming an undeniable reality: "I will build my church, and the gates of hell shall not prevail against it" (Matt. 16:18 KJV).

Since Satan is unable to quench with persecution the fires of revival that prayer ignites, he relentlessly tries to smother the divine spark of redemptive intercession that is flickering in the soul of every child of God. That heavenly ember glows deep in the heart of each true believer. The call to world-altering, kingdom-advancing prayer is a universal calling given to *every* child of God. God infuses this calling to prayer into the redeemed soul at the moment of spiritual rebirth.

As was His death, the entire life of Jesus was an intercession for lost humanity. Even now, at the right hand of God, Jesus ever lives to make intercession for us. This *Interceding Jesus* dwells in the heart of every person who has been born of God. We are the sons and daughters of God. We are partakers of the divine nature. At the moment we were born again, our spirit inherited in its very nature the call to interceding prayer for the advancement of God's kingdom on the earth. The calling of Jesus to redemptive intercession is inherent in every child of God. The vocation of intercession is innate because it is indelibly written on the spiritual DNA of every blood-bought soul, including yours and mine!

Prayer is Our Primary Vocation

Since prayer is the primary vocation and the most solemn duty of every child of God, it is a tragedy of eternal consequence when this holy calling is neglected. It is our privilege and responsibility to intercede before God in order to secure the grace of redemption for fallen humankind in every generation. Indeed, there has never been a time in the history of the church when the apostolic foundation of corporate prayer revealed in the book of Acts has been more needed, yet more neglected, than it is right now. The popular American church culture is not conducive to cultivating the prevailing corporate prayer that birthed and empowered the first-century church. What is prevailing in the modern American church is a man-pleasing message that focuses on our individual needs and desires.

The first century church embraced a gospel that called believers to lay down their lives for the advancement of God's kingdom. She dedicated herself to God in prayer as believers labored together in a heavenly calling much larger than their individual dreams and ambitions. Certainly God enriches every soul that is born into the family of God. However, the popular gospel of today, which focuses on the personal fulfillment of individual believers, hinders the advancement of God's kingdom. Multitudes that gather in our houses of worship week after week remain captivated by a partial gospel that rarely challenges the hearers to escape from deceptive paradigms of self. A continual focus on God blessing our individual lives obscures God's expectations for our devotion to corporate responsibility. This leads to a self-serving brand of Christianity that concentrates on personal hopes and dreams rather than on embracing God's call to sacrifice self in order to advance God's dream of humankind's redemption, revival, and reformation.

The ultimate intercession that Jesus agonizingly endured at Calvary can only reach broken humanity in a fallen world through the redemptive intercession of His people. Yet too often our inborn spark of redemptive intercession is smothered with self, stifled with religious activity, or extinguished with worldly distractions. Are you willing to have that divine flicker rekindled until your soul is ablaze in passionate prayer? Will you allow the redeeming love of Jesus to flow through *you* in prayer to release God's power in this desperate generation?

It takes only one spark to ignite a fire that could consume a city. Will you invite the Holy Spirit to fan the divine spark of redemptive intercession within you until the flames of fervent prayer are glowing in your heart, ignited in your church, and burning in your region? Do not underestimate the divine possibilities your prayers could release. From your heart to the hearts of your friends and family, from church to church, and from city to city, your prayers could torch a great American awakening. Fuel the flames of redemptive intercession in your soul! Fall on your knees and pray!

That which has been done in spiritual matters can be done again, and be better done. This was Christ's view. He said, "Verily, verily, I say unto you, He that believeth on me, the works that I do shall he do also; and greater works than these shall he do; because I go unto my Father." The past has not exhausted the possibilities, nor the demands, for doing great things for God. The church that is dependent on its past history for its miracles of power and grace is a fallen church.

—E. M. Bounds

Heaven is full of answers to prayer for which no one ever bothered to ask.

—Billy Graham

Since the days of Pentecost, has the whole church ever put aside every other work and waited upon Him for ten days that the Spirit's power might be manifested? We give too much attention to method and machinery and resources and too little to the Source of power.

—Hudson Taylor

Chapter 8

MIRACLE
RELEASING PRAYER

And when they had prayed, the place where they were assembled together was shaken; and they were all filled with the Holy Spirit, and they spoke the word of God with boldness.... And with great power the apostles gave witness to the resurrection of the Lord Jesus. And great grace was upon them all.

—Acts 4:31, 33

HOW DESPERATE THE American church is to embrace a revelation of the miraculous, earthshaking, hell-invading prayer ministry of the first century church. That divine revelation is indelibly engraved on the pages of the New Testament and irrefutably amplified by the lives of those believers who were living epistles of prayer in the book of Acts.

Apprehending the supernatural spiritual realities of New Testament Christianity that graced the early church is impossible without the inclusion of vibrant prayer. The world-altering power that surged through first century Christianity will be rediscovered by the twenty-first century church when corporate prayer for the advancement of God's kingdom is widely included as an imperative foundation of church life and practice.

Prayer Works Miracles

Any serious study of the miracles of Jesus reveals an unquestionable link between His life devoted to prayer and all of the grace and gifts that flowed through Him day by day as He miraculously touched broken humanity. His daily impact on the lives of people was rooted in long nights of prayer as He lingered in empowering communion with His heavenly Father. Observing the prayer life of Jesus and the signs and wonders that accompanied Him, His apostles led the early church as they followed the same heavenly blueprint of fervent, relentless prayer, with the same supernatural results.

The very first meeting of the church after the ascension of Jesus was a ten day prayer meeting, where one hundred and twenty believers gathered together in an upper room in Jerusalem. Heaven's response to the church's first gathering of united intercession was a miraculous outpouring of the Holy Spirit. Those who had assembled to seek God in the upper room were *all* filled with the Holy Spirit and began to glorify God, speaking in other tongues.

Emboldened with supernatural power, Peter preached to the crowd that had come to Jerusalem for the Jewish Feast of Pentecost. Peter proclaimed boldly that Jesus had risen from the dead and that God had made Him both Lord and Christ. Then He admonished them:

> *Repent, and let every one of you be baptized in the name of Jesus Christ for the remission of sins; and you shall receive the gift of the Holy Spirit.*

(Acts 2:38)

This verse reveals the three foundations for building a personal spiritual life: repentance, baptism of the believer, and receiving the gift of the Holy Spirit. As a result of this Pentecostal sermon, three thousand souls were added to the infant church that day. These new converts continued steadfastly in four things: the apostles' doctrine, fellowship, breaking of bread, and prayers (Acts 2:42). This verse in the genesis chapter of the New Testament church lucidly gives us the four apostolic foundations for establishing a vibrant community of believers.

The New American Standard Bible says, "They were continually devoting themselves" to these four foundations of community life. Tracing church life throughout the sacred record reveals that corporate prayer was one of the four primary foundations believers practiced in the first century church. This vital truth is an undeniable fact that the entire book of Acts authenticates. Meetings of fervent, incessant prayer were prevalent in the gatherings of the early church. Regular sessions of persevering prayer wherever the church met were then, and should now be, a vital foundation of normal church life. In light of the Scriptural prototype of the first century, church life practiced without the apostolic foundation of fervent, corporate prayer is a frail substitute for biblical Christianity. Clearly, the noblest human efforts will never produce divine results. Prayer is the only God-ordained link between everything believers on earth need for advancing the church and heaven's empowering response. When the church fails to pray, the church fails in its very mission on the earth.

Prayer is the foundation of miraculous, divine intervention. After the man was healed at the Gate Beautiful, the religious leaders commanded the apostles "not to speak at all nor teach in the name of Jesus" (Acts 4:18). In response to the threats of religious leaders, the united believers lifted their voices together as they beseeched God for miraculous signs and wonders.

And being let go, they went to their own companions and reported all that the chief priests and elders had said to them. So when they heard that, they raised their voice to God with one accord.... Now, Lord, look on their threats, and grant to Your servants that with all boldness they may speak Your word, by stretching out Your hand to heal, and that signs and wonders may be done through the name of Your holy Servant Jesus.

(Acts 4:23–24, 29–30)

Their confident appeal for miracles as they lifted their voices together in prayer brought heaven's swift response.

And when they had prayed, the place where they were assembled together was shaken; and they were all filled with the Holy Spirit, and they spoke the word of God with boldness.... And with great power the apostles gave witness to the resurrection of the Lord Jesus. And great grace was upon them all.

(Acts 4:31, 33)

The miraculous ministry that prayer was fueling accelerated after the death of Ananias and Sapphira.

And through the hands of the apostles many signs and wonders were done among the people. And they were all with one accord in Solomon's Porch. Yet none of the rest dared join them, but the people esteemed them highly. And believers were increasingly added to the Lord, multitudes of both men and women, so that they brought the sick out into the streets and laid them on beds and couches, that at least the shadow of Peter passing by might fall on some of them. Also a multitude gathered from the surrounding cities to Jerusalem, bringing sick people and those who were tormented by unclean spirits, and they were all healed.

(Acts 5:12–16)

Prayer Releases God's Power

God's miraculous intervention in response to His church united in fervent prayer is eternally chronicled throughout the divine Scriptures that form the historical record of first century Christianity. The Book of Acts is the heavenly blueprint that reveals God's willingness to intervene miraculously whenever

Christians unite in fervent prayer to advance God's Kingdom. This blueprint of the praying church and heaven's glorious response is not something that God intended we would just reverently admire as biblical history. Christians united in prayer can always obtain miraculous power to make history!

"The church that is dependent on its past history for its miracles of power and grace is a fallen church." These are very insightful words written long ago by E. M. Bounds. Christians in every generation should experience miracles of power and grace. The pattern of prayer revealed in Acts should be emulated with passion and perseverance until God's kingdom-advancing miracles grace the American church of the twenty-first century.

If ever there was a generation that needed the miraculous intervention of God, it is our own. Clearly, our unchangeable God has not changed, but the dynamic prayer ministry that adorned the early church with the power of the miraculous is missing in this age. Still, if Christians would unite in ardent gatherings of prayer, the heavens would soon open with manifestations of God's power.

Even now, a fallen world is languishing under sin's debilitating curse. Lost humanity sits devastated, waiting for grace that can only be obtained by the praying church. Will we pray until the heavens open and God releases miracles of liberating light and power in the midst of this darkened age? If not, then multitudes of lost souls will wait in vain for prayers that we will never pray. *God forbid! Almighty God, wash our lethargic souls of our wretched sin of prayerless indifference!*

God's Power Never Waned

God always intended that prayer would be the primary work of His church. Jesus told us that seeking His Kingdom should be our number one priority in life. "But seek first the

Kingdom of God" (Matt. 6:33). In partnership with God's Spirit, the church's prayer ministry was predestined to release heaven's miraculous power in every generation. Tragically, we have abandoned the pristine depths of life-giving prayer. To our own detriment we have chosen to be mired in the murky shallows of impotent human effort. As a result, man's carnal cunning has usurped the unsearchable wisdom of God.

We engage the mind but neglect the heart. We deny the Holy Spirit complete access to expose and transform us inwardly into the very image of Christ. *That* transformation would empower us to pray with kingdom authority and world-altering power. Adrift in a fog of self-reliance, the church has substituted entertaining programs for God's liberating power and traded manifestations of the miraculous for crowd gathering techniques. It would be impossible to articulate prayer's limitless potential—or overstate its immeasurable worth. Heaven's storehouse of miracles is always full! It was not depleted by the first century church. The power of our omnipotent God has never waned. What did wane was the fervent prayer of the church, which summoned God's miraculous intervention into the affairs of men and nations. It is an eternal truth that the God of the Bible is a miracle working God: "Jesus Christ is the same yesterday, today, and forever" (Heb. 13:8).

Christ's miracles never ceased. What did cease was the passionate prayer ministry of His church that moved heaven to release the miraculous among men. We are not dealing with an almighty God who is selfish and reluctant to intervene supernaturally in the affairs of men. Instead, God Almighty is dealing with a self-centered church that is reluctant to pray sacrificially for the advancement of God's kingdom in this me-first generation. Will the twenty-first century American church ever break free from America's culture of humanism and give selfless prayer the place of preeminence it held in the life and ministry of first century Christianity? More directly to the point, *will you?*

In light of the early church's effervescent wellspring of prayer, our brief moments of silence, with bowed heads and doubting hearts, and the obligatory, frail ramblings often offered to God from our polished pulpits are beggarly at best. Do we actually think that this level of superficial praying could possibly suffice in these grave moments in the United States' history? Are we unaware of America's great spiritual peril? Will the indifferent church ever understand that while she is sleeping in denial, the powers of hell are winning the war against the very foundations of western Christian civilization?

The only weapon capable of overcoming hell's vicious onslaught against Christianity is the church united in God-moving, hell-shaking prayer. Nothing else can apprehend the supernatural power of God. Thanks be to God! He has given us a biblical model of the church united in one accord, demonstrating the astonishing force of kingdom-advancing prayer. The God who so willingly answered the prayers that ascended heavenward from the first century church is waiting for us to join together in prayer to invoke heaven's astounding power in this generation. If the twenty-first century church unites to pray with the same commitment and passion that the first century church demonstrated, our intercessions will triumph over the prevailing darkness of our times as God miraculously births the dawning of an American awakening.

Are you listening to God as He tries to awaken your slumbering heart? The Holy Spirit is calling you to join this great cause. Nothing less than America's future and the eternal destiny of millions of souls are at stake.

The heavens are pregnant with miracles of divine intervention destined for this desperate generation. Heavenly hosts are poised in reverent readiness, but they are restrained from release by our appalling sin of prayerlessness. Will the eternal pages of history record a twenty-first century eruption of kingdom-advancing prayer that apprehended heaven's power to redeem multitudes and heal the nations? If not, then prayerlessness will have aborted God's highest purpose for His church in our generation and detonated the implosion of western Christian civilization into a new dark age.

May it never be that *our* lethargy and disobedience sealed the fate of unredeemed billions in today's world because they could not be reached by a self-enthroned, enfeebled, prayerless church! Church of God, flee from this paralyzing stupor! Get up from your comfortable beds of spiritual ease and run to the altars of selfless intercession. United, on our knees, our prayers will invoke the God of heaven and earth to intervene in the affairs of our fallen, desperately needy nation and the entire world. With God, all things are possible. Without Him, America does not have a prayer!

There has never been a spiritual awakening in any country or locality that did not begin in united prayer.

—A. T. Pierson

To look back upon the progress of the divine Kingdom upon earth is to review revival periods which have come like refreshing showers upon dry and thirsty ground, making the desert to blossom as the rose, and bringing new eras of spiritual life and activity just when the church had fallen under the influence of the apathy of the times, and needed to be aroused to a new sense of her duty and responsibility....Every mighty move of the Spirit of God has had its source in the prayer chamber.

—E. M. Bounds

Chapter 9

SEEDS FOR THE RESTORATION OF THE NATIONS

If My people who are called by My name will humble themselves, and pray and seek My face, and turn from their wicked ways, then I will hear from heaven, and will forgive their sin and heal their land.

—2 Chronicles 7:14

WHAT A MIRACULOUS promise! The healing of our land is much more than a divine possibility. It is God's glorious intention to intervene in the affairs of nations to heal and to restore. Our God, the Creator of heaven and earth, has bound Himself to His Word. There are no variables in this text that could leave us wavering in doubt about God's gracious intent. There is not even the faintest hint of any divine reluctance.

God has fully committed Himself and all of heaven's resources to doing exactly what He said He would do. His promise is indelibly etched on the sacred pages of the eternal text. "God is not a man that He should lie" (Num. 23:19). "Forever, O Lord, Your word is settled in heaven" (Ps. 119:89). Why then has God's promise to heal our land been restrained on the earth? The healing of our land can only be secured if God's people fulfill His conditions on their knees. We are required to pray. Nothing but a great movement of repentance and prayer throughout the church in America will meet God's requirements to obtain this nation-altering promise.

For millennia, God has stored in 2 Chronicles 7:14 the choice seeds of divine promise for healing the nations of the world. Endued with power by the Creator, these potent grains possess the inherent gift of releasing all of heaven's vast resources to meet the desperate spiritual needs of fallen humankind in a rebellious world. Permitted to take root and grow, the life force within these kernels of truth could enable the twenty-first century church to cultivate divine visitations of mercy and healing throughout the nations of the world. Empowered by obedience to the conditions of heaven's limitless promise, the praying church could rise up to reap an unprecedented harvest of souls.

Yet, before the vast potential in these tiny seeds will ever flourish, these living grains of the world's hope must be sown and planted deeply in the fertile soil of willing hearts. They must take root in the warm, moist souls of those who are bowed in humility at the feet of Jesus. We need to hear with our hearts the divine declaration reverberating down through the centuries with all of the power and authority of God Almighty, who decreed:

If My people who are called by My name will humble themselves, and pray, and seek My face, and turn from their wicked ways, then I will hear from heaven, and will forgive their sin and heal their land.

If the church at large in America would walk in the conditions God has prescribed in this lone scripture, glorious healing would spring up speedily in our land! Well-watered with the tearful intercessions of a praying multitude, these seeds of promise would germinate and quickly grow into a revival of authentic biblical spirituality. Each of these vigorous seeds, planted in a surrendered soul, would yield thirty, sixty, or a hundredfold. As they matured in heart after heart, in church after church, and in city after city, this revival of prayer would bloom into an American awakening and mature into a cultural reformation.

Tragically, in most of God's children's hearts, these seeds lie dormant and uncultivated, withering in the arid wilderness of worldly distractions and spiritual indifference. While our fallen Christian nation languishes under the demonic tyranny of sin's barren darkness and our culture plummets into unprecedented moral degradation, God's promise to heal our land rests completely on our obedience to His terms of clemency. In God's mercy, the condition of the land has absolutely nothing to do with the fulfillment of the promise to heal it. It is God's people alone who hold the future of the United States in their hands. At this crucial moment in American history, God is calling His church to plant the seeds of national healing, to be reaped by our children and all future generations of Americans. Only His nationwide church, mobilized in prayer, can cultivate the seeds of a national awakening and spiritual restoration.

Will You Answer God's Call?

Have the glorious seeds of world-altering prayer been lying dormant and uncultivated in your own soul? If so, repent and join the multitudes of believers who are answering God's call to give themselves to God in prayer for national repentance and an American awakening. Now is the time for all Christians from every denomination to labor together in the fields of intercession. If we unite on our knees, we will sow the seeds of national repentance that will blossom into a sweeping revival and a glorious, divine visitation. Only the seeds of prayer sown by the multi-denominational body of Christ hold the promise of the spiritual rebirth of America and the hope of a cultural reformation. Will you embrace this promise and humble yourself in prayer? God forbid that America's hope would be aborted by a prayerless church! In the life-or-death struggle for the heart and soul of America, child of God, choose life! *Fall on your knees and pray!*

The divine proclamation of truth in this scripture requires no great biblical expositor to interpret its meaning. No eloquent oratory is necessary to illuminate such a straightforward text. This plain, unadorned verse is not veiled in obscure, allegorical verbiage, nor is it hidden in the complexities of the original language that only doctors of theology could possibly comprehend. The revelation of what God requires from each one of us is unmistakably clear, and the results of our obedience to His expectations are clearer still. The nationwide church united in prayer would bring healing to our spiritually devastated land! It is prayer and *only prayer* that can revive the complacent church in America, save the lost souls of multitudes doomed to eternal damnation without Christ, rebuild the eroded spiritual foundations of our Christ-centered national heritage, and begin the reformation of our reprobate culture.

For decades 2 Chronicles 7:14 has been proclaimed from the pulpits of the American church. Yet, *listening* to sermons and studying this scripture will not suffice. Only *obedience* to the divine precepts this scripture teaches will release God's blessing. It is self-evident that the church at large has not met the clear but costly conditions that would secure the promised healing of our land.

American Christians *know* this verse. Many have memorized it. In choruses we have sung it. We put it on car bumpers, print it on posters, and engrave it on plaques. We read it in our church bulletins and discuss it during Sunday school. We wear it on T-shirts and embroider it on hats. We have done everything but give ourselves humbly to God in repentance and selfless prayer to obey it.

Our annual prayer breakfasts and yearly days of prayer do little more than salve the conscience of the church that God is urgently trying to rouse. Prayer must become the primary focus of the American church. All Christian prayer has value, but a word of prayer or a day of prayer will never meet the costly requirements revealed in this verse. If the American church at large applies herself with all spiritual diligence to meet God's conditions, then God will fulfill His Word and unlock His astounding promise. If we humbly and honestly invite the Holy Spirit to search our souls, the simplicity of the inspired words in this verse will reveal the spiritual apathy residing in our own deceived hearts. Prayerless indifference has kept God's church from aligning with His will. Only the nationwide church, united on her knees, can meet the prerequisites that will miraculously release God's extraordinary pledge to heal our land.

There is no great mystery hidden in this scripture. Instead, these God-breathed words expose the mystery of the church's sin of prayerlessness. Our death of passionate intercession for the spiritual rebirth of our fallen Christian nation reveals how far American Christians have drifted from the God who has ordained prayer—*much* prayer—fervent, unceasing, prevailing prayer as the greatest work and the most solemn duty of all who believe. The mystery of prayerlessness and the absence of world-impacting prayer are irrefutable evidence that proves we are guilty beyond any reasonable doubt. The church in prayerless indifference shares the guilt for the sins of our nation.

The American church has fallen woefully short of the glory of God and chosen a life sentence of spiritual frailty and cultural impotence. *God, have mercy on us!* Only repentance will cleanse our souls from their prideful self-reliance and set us free from this prison of spiritual mediocrity. If we repent, God will terminate our sentence and grant each one of us a full pardon!

The story has often been told of a young lad who believed he had figured out a way to confound the village wise man.

Holding a tiny dove asleep in his hands, he came to the old man. Boastfully, the lad asked, "Is this dove dead or alive?" The wise man immediately realized that if he said the little dove was alive, the boy would crush it in his hands and kill it. If he said it was dead, the lad would release the dove and let it fly heavenward. Looking first at the sleeping dove, and then into the eyes of the child, the wise man softly answered, "The answer to that question rests completely in your hands."

The destiny of our nation rests completely in the hands of God's church. Will the right to life ever prevail over our vile culture of death? The answer to that question rests completely in the hands of God's church. Will America reap the consequences owed for her grievous sin, or will she find God's mercy in national repentance? The answer to that question rests completely in the hands of the church.

Now, at the final crossroads of revival or ruin, which road will America choose? The answer to this question rests completely in the hands of God's church. Will you let your heart fly heavenward in fervent prayer for the spiritual rebirth of America, or will you crush the tender stirrings of the Holy Spirit? The answer to that question rests completely in your hands. Answer wisely.

The true man of God is heartsick, grieved at the worldliness of the church, grieved at the blindness of the church, grieved at the corruption in the church, grieved at the toleration of sin in the church, grieved at the prayerlessness in the church. He is disturbed that the corporate prayer of the church no longer pulls down the strongholds of the devil. He is embarrassed that the church folks no longer cry in their despair before a devil-ridden, sin-mad society, "Why could we not cast him out" (Matthew 17:19).

—Leonard Ravenhill

Chapter 10

THE HOUSE OF PRAYER FOR ALL NATIONS

> *Even them I will bring to My holy mountain, and make them joyful in My house of prayer. Their burnt offerings and their sacrifices will be accepted on My altar; for My house shall be called a house of prayer for all nations.*
>
> —Isaiah 56:7

HEAVEN IS MYSTIFIED by the days, weeks, months, and years of prayerless silence that is pervasive in the modern American church. This heartbreaking hush hinders heaven from releasing the all-encompassing grace of redemptive restoration into the affairs of humankind in one nation under God. All the while, in silent restraint, legions of angels stand poised, waiting to respond swiftly should our voices ascend to God with one accord in prayer. If it were possible, the God of Wonders Himself would have to wonder at the deafening quiet He incredibly endures as He looks down, week after week, month after month, and year after year, upon the empty altars, in the empty sanctuaries, in the empty buildings we call churches.

How in God's name can His people remain mute in prayerless indifference as the very foundations of Christian civilization are relentlessly besieged? Is the church so cocooned in the complacency of comfortable religion that she is oblivious to the fact that hell is waging an all-out war against the church? Where, in God's name, are those with spiritual perception who understand that prayer is America's only hope for a spiritual awakening and a cultural reformation?

Will the buildings that house His church across America ever truly become a "house of prayer for all nations"? If not, then our only other option is to ignore God's nation-altering and world-awakening promise of heaven-sent healing, revealed in 2 Chronicles. Thereby we will seal our dreadful fate of ever-worsening national depravity in an anti-Christian culture and the ever-nearing black night of America's ominous reckoning for our national slaughter of the poor innocents. *May almighty God forbid!*

Rather, let us return to God with obedient hearts and build tens of thousands of altars of fervent, public prayer in our houses of worship. It is not too late. Our God is "slow to anger" (Ps. 145:8). He is gracious—and full of compassion and mercy. With repentance, this mercy can save a nation from reaping the destruction its wickedness has sown. There still is hope that God will cleanse and restore *one nation under God.*

> *The instant I speak concerning a nation and concerning a kingdom, to pluck up, to pull down, and to destroy it, if that nation against whom I have spoken turns from its evil, I will relent of the disaster that I thought to bring upon it.*
>
> (Jer. 18:7–8)

Tragically, that hope is lying dormant in the barren, spiritual womb of a silent, prayerless church. God's unmet conditions in His promise to heal our land are not hidden in perplexing parables or sealed in symbolic scriptural mysteries. Leaving no doubt as to God's expectations, they are explicitly revealed in 2 Chronicles 7:14. The divine healing and spiritual restoration of our nation requires nothing more than the obedience of His children to humble themselves, pray, seek His face, and turn from their wicked ways. This promise has not been fulfilled because God's people have not responded to the call by falling on their knees.

The depth of the depravity of the lost in America and the spiritual condition of our blood-guilty land has absolutely nothing to do with obtaining the promise of God's healing. Our fallen nation reflects the tragic fall of God's glorious church from her throne of world-swaying prayer into the impotence of prayerless self-reliance and self-absorbed indifference. American society has not plummeted so far into sin that Lady Liberty is beyond the grasp of a loving and forgiving God. If we who believe would repent and present ourselves as living sacrifices in selfless intercession before Him, God's fire would soon fall and ignite the flames of a sweeping revival, leading to national repentance. God's clarion call in 2 Chronicles 7:14 places the entire responsibility of seizing the promise of healing our land squarely on the shoulders of His people. If the church at large would unite in prayer, we would obtain His divine favor, release His unmerited mercies, and invoke all of heaven's power to secure a divine visitation for our wayward country. This spiritual awakening would reform the twenty-first century church, release God's promise to heal our land, and begin the restoration of one nation under God. Heart by heart, church by church, and city by city—may we become His "house of prayer for all nations."

With the great promises of 2 Chronicles 7:14 encouraging us to seek God's face, why have so many believers chosen not to bow in obedience to rebuild the altars of fervent prayer and selfless intercession? Perhaps we are too preoccupied with this life's pleasures and earthly pursuits to give ourselves to God in earnest, pleading for souls. Where are the congregations of saints that linger long in self-sacrificing prayer? Have our forms of Christianity in this age become so overtly personal and self-serving that we shun seeking the advancement of God's kingdom? When did we forget that *prayer* is the first and foremost calling of every member of God's church in every generation? Jesus told us, "But seek first the kingdom of God" (Matt. 6:33).

Perhaps the mesmerizing enchantments of worldly distractions have captured our sluggish souls. Has pleasure so ensnared us that we excuse ourselves from discharging our solemn duty of seeking God in prayer? It is apparent by our prayerlessness that our secular culture has so sculpted modern Christianity into its own image and likeness that the vision to shape the destiny of nations through united prayer has been chiseled from the heart and soul of the church. The dimension of passionate, prevailing prayer that could release heaven's power into the affairs of nations is foreign to most of God's people in the American church. This same church boisterously laments the day when prayer was removed from our public schools, while, without so much as a whimper, the altars of world-altering prayer were first eradicated from the church.

It is terrifying to face the truth, so we ignore it. Multiple millions of professing Christians are oblivious to America's grave peril of impending judgment, while a plague of prayerlessness proves that millions of others who claim Christ as their Savior just do not care. The spiritual condition of our nation is nothing more than the telling reflection of the impoverished prayer ministry of His apathetic church. While the church world bewails the condition of America's anti-Christian culture, heaven wails, weeping over the prayerlessness in the church that allowed it to happen—and the spiritual indifference that continues to tolerate it!

Still, it is not too late! The expiration date on this promise of healing our land has not passed. Our nation is not so sick that God's promise to heal it would fail! If the national church will mobilize, in obedience to the biblical precepts revealed in this one short verse, God will visit our nation and usher in the greatest revival and cultural reformation in the history of the world. Conversely, without the restraining influence and offensive power of the churches in America uniting in prayer, evil will continue its deadly assault and ultimately triumph completely over what little remains of Christian reality in the public life of the United States.

God forbid we should neglect to pray for mercy before it is too late, thereby surrendering the future of the United States into the hands of Christ's malignant adversary. The Scriptures are clear. God has already assigned His mission of world-impacting prayer to everyone who believes on His Son, Jesus. Will you surrender yourself in obedience to God to pursue your high calling and fulfill your solemn duty to intercede? In revival or in ruin, the destiny of America will be eternally linked to your decision. In the name of Jesus, I beseech you to choose wisely—*fall on your knees, and pray!*

For further information on the ministry of American Patriots in Prayer, please contact:

David Hamer
American Patriots in Prayer
1616 East Griffin Parkway
#190
Mission, Texas 78576

www.patriotsinprayer.org
email: dave@patriotsinprayer.org

Printed in the United States
139289LV00002B/1/P